The Todmorden Book of the Dead

John Morrison

Pick the bones out of *that*...

Dedicated to D, in a forlorn and hopeless kind of way.

Thanks to Gary Thomas for the brilliant cover picture (with a tip of the hat to Albrecht Dürer) and to Mike Barrett for pulling it all together.

John Morrison

john@trunorth.demon.co.uk

Published by Mutton Stew

26 New Road, Hebden Bridge, West Yorkshire HX7 8EF

Copyright © John Morrison 2002

ISBN: 0-9538608-1-7

Cover picture by Gary Thomas (01706 817681)

Designed by Mike Barrett (mike@frogsdesign.co.uk)

Printed by Intype, Wimbledon

Contents

Looks like rain	5
Fun and games	11
On Heartbreak Hill	17
Dog day afternoon	22
Ravages of time	30
Highdays and holidays	44
On the buses	55
Saint Bernard's head	60
Right to roam	64

Looks like rain

The weather is a staple of casual conversation in Milltown. This isn't the city, where people pass on the street without a word or a nod. In a small town, with everyone knowing each other, a chance meeting demands a response. But we still don't have the time to stand around and gossip. Not all of us, anyway. So what's needed is a simple, formulaic exchange that allows us to inquire briefly about one another's welfare, and then move on.

So the reply to the question "How are things?" is "Fine, thanks", or "Mustn't grumble", or, at a pinch, "This cold snap's playing havoc with my arthritis". The question is rhetorical. The shorter the answer, the better; there's no need for a long list of seasonal complaints. So a glaringly obvious remark about the weather is a better way to achieve conversational closure ("Turned out nice again". "Pah! It didn't even turn out nice the *first* time").

But, my, how things have changed. Just when we thought we'd got Mother Nature under control and walking to heel, she starts fighting back. And not just with a nip on the ankle, either; we're getting a comprehensive savaging. We watch – with a mixture of awe and astonishment – as our weather takes an apocalyptic turn.

We used to tune into the weather forecast if we were planning a day out, and the farmers would pay particular heed at hay time. But the weather never dominated our lives in the way it does today. Now we huddle round the radio, like folk did in the war, to hear the latest news from the front. Will it be warm, cold, or maybe just occluded? We listen intently to the forecasts, even though a lot of them seem like guesswork. After all, isn't "a 50% chance of rain" just a fancy way of saying "We haven't the foggiest"? It doesn't answer the burning question: do we need to take an umbrella or not?

The prophets of doom talk about climate change. Here in the South Pennines we were surprised to have a climate at all; we thought we just had weather. And mostly lousy weather at that. But even the experts can't agree about what the future holds. A few years back, during a spate of especially cold winters, we were chipping dogs off lamp-posts. On the flimsiest of evidence – 'a cold snap', for God's sake – the climatologists insisted we were heading towards another Ice Age. That chilly prognosis has been conveniently forgotten; now it's global warming that's all the rage.

That's the problem with climatologists. The only way they can get their research grants renewed is to come up with ever more outlandish forecasts. A cataclysmic meteor shower is thirty million years overdue, we're told, though who knows what the residents of a small South Pennine milltown are supposed to do with this kind of information. The world could be wiped out, apparently, just like that. It could be any time now. Is there really any point in collecting any more air miles? Maybe we should just stay home and take refuge beneath the kitchen table.

Though the climate doesn't actually *feel* any warmer – this is Pennine Yorkshire, after all – it's certainly unpredictable. The stakes have been raised. We used to have rain; now we have storms. We used to have wind; now, bizarrely, we have twisters and tornadoes. We used to have dry spells; now we have droughts that empty reservoirs and transform green lawns into tawny tundra. We keep a snow shovel by the bedside, in case we need to dig our way out. If there's a pattern to our weather, then we haven't detected it. All bets are off. Anything can happen.

The *Milltown Times* tries to keep us informed about the weather. It would be good to have advance warning of storms – giving the emergency services the chance to evacuate people, shore up buildings and bring trees indoors. However, the paper's budget can't run to any forecasting equipment more sophisticated than a piece of wet string hung outside the office window. So instead of telling us what weather we can look forward to next week, the paper harnesses the power of hindsight to tell us what the weather was like *last* week.

Over the years, the weather has been kind to Old Ted. Long retired, he props up the bar at the Crown, regaling our more gullible visitors with tall tales of weird weather phenomena - culled from memory, his overactive imagination and the pages of Old Moore's Almanac. Once he heard a cuckoo in March: unheard of. Except it wasn't a cuckoo. And it wasn't March either.

Ted remembers a traveller who, having got lost one night during a particularly savage blizzard, tied up his horse to what he assumed was a hitching-post. Next morning, when the the snow had melted, he found his horse hanging from the top of the church steeple. Incredible... Whirlwinds would regularly pick up chicken coops, cars – even houses – and deposit them miles away, in some other town, without a scratch. Amazing... If the visitors are sufficiently impressed by Ted's tall tales to buy him a drink ("I'll have a pint of the strong stuff. And a whisky chaser. And one of those slim panatellas. Cheers"), where's the harm in that?

Now, though, we get weird weather all the time, and Ted's stories don't draw the crowds like they used to. Visitors steal his thunder with experiences of their own. "What a coincidence!", they say. "The very same thing happened to *us*, not half an hour ago". Ted cuts a forlorn figure these days, harassing visitors with his irrelevant observations. If he says "Aren't these fine buttocks for an old man?" one more time, the landlord is going to have to throw him out.

Here we are again, approaching another Pennine winter with a dawn chorus of hacking coughs. The recent floods have left everyone feeling twitchy; Milltown looks like Sandbag City. Those of us who waded through our homes, knee-deep in muddy water, will never look at rain in quite the same way again. We used to enjoy the percussion of raindrops on the roof. It was vaguely comforting, especially when we were snug and warm inside our little terraced houses. But not any more. Now the rain sounds like the beating of war drums, as the Zulus laid siege to Rourkes Drift. It's disturbing.[1]

We used to pull the curtains every evening, and bolt our doors, secure in the knowledge that we'd locked out most of life's unpleasantness. We could sleep soundly in our beds, untroubled by thoughts of intruders. But, as we've discovered from painful experience, there's not a lot we can do to keep floodwater out. The sandbags may look business-like, but they're about as much use as the pills that Dr Madeley hands out to the most persistent malingerers who fill up his waiting room. An Englishman's home may be his castle, but right now it feels as though we're living in the moat.

Whenever the town darkens beneath a bank of storm-clouds, and the river threatens once again to burst its banks, a little group of cagoule-clad locals convenes in silence on the old packhorse bridge. They glare balefully down into the swollen river, hoping to bring down the water level by will-power alone. At moments like this the Bahamas have never looked so enticing... or so very, very far away.

What have we done to deserve all this rain? Have we made the gods angry? If so, what will the next affliction be? Well, if Bob the postman is anything to go by, it could be a plague of boils. This

---

[1] Ah, yes, the floods. Water issued - like some Biblical miracle - from pipes and culverts and holes in stone walls. The swollen river surged intemperately past the old packhorse bridge, the water the colour of stewed tea. With the ground waterlogged, and the rain incessant, there was nowhere for all that water to go. Something had to give. Old Ted was one of many householders who came downstairs the following morning to find muddy brown furniture floating around his sitting room... and loan-sharks swimming about outside. "What's this?", said Ted, as a man in a suit and, incongruously, a pair of wellington boots slipped Ted his business card. "I just want to help", the man replied. "You want to help?", said Ted. "Then grab a mop and a bucket and help me get some of this water out". "I didn't mean that kind of help". "No, I know you didn't. Now fuck off, there's a good lad, I've got work to do."

The police blew up their inflatable dinghy; they'd never had occasion to use it before. With the put-put-put of the outboard motor the only noise to be heard, they pootled rather self-consciously around the flooded streets of Milltown. There can have been only one possible purpose to their perambulations: to be able to tell their grandchildren about the time they pootled around the flooded streets of Milltown in an inflatable dinghy.

It took Ted a few weeks to get over the trauma. Looking on the bright side, it was the first time that the soft furnishings in Riverside Cottage had been colour-coordinated. But Ted saw red when his Council Tax went up, on the basis that he now had an indoor pool. Where, pray, was the justice in that?

isn't something he's keen to talk about, even to Dr Madeley. *Especially* to Dr Madeley. But there's a lot of legwork involved in a rural round. After delivering his letters, all Bob wants is to sit down, put his feet up and read the *Milltown Times* from cover to cover. For the last few days, though, even this simple pleasure has been denied him.

Left to his own devices, Bob would probably just suffer in silence. That's a man's attitude to illness in a nutshell: ignore it, and maybe it will go away of its own accord. It's the same attitude that Bob has adopted with all the vehicles he's ever owned, which is why he's never managed to sell any car for more than half what he paid for it. Due to his parsimonious use of engine oil (always a false economy, as his wife Cath keeps reminding him), Bob didn't make a penny when he got rid of his last motor. Worse, he had to pay the guy from the breaker's yard to tow it away.

Once Cath had found out what was troubling Bob – by conducting a discreet, fact-finding, night-time, finger-tip search beneath the duvet – she packed him off to see the doctor. Bob knew she was right (as she keeps reminding him) but felt obliged to give a convincing show of reluctance. His immediate fears were unfounded, thankfully, the waiting room being so full that he had to stand.

At this time of year there are plenty of people in Milltown who are happy to spend quality time in a friendly, germ-laden environment. Old biddies, mostly. What's the point in cranking the central heating up at home, when the doctor's waiting room is so warm and welcoming? There are dog-eared magazines to read, full of recipes and knitting patterns. There's a tank of tropical fish: more entertaining than the daytime TV they'd be watching if they were at home. Apart from Countdown, of course, and that nice Richard Whiteley.

There used to be a machine that dispensed hot coffee until Dr Madeley twigged why he was dealing with an outbreak of scalded lips and fingers. Yes, if these hypochondriacs aren't ill when they arrive at the surgery, they've usually managed to pick up a sniffle – or better – by the time they leave.

Dr Madeley can only spare about five minutes per patient, before writing a prescription for some harmless, sugar-coated placebo. This is what a lot of doctors seem to have forgotten. Older people want someone to listen to them, to take their problems seriously. They appreciate a doctor who will lean back in his swivel chair, press his fingertips together and nod empathetically. Someone prepared to give his undivided attention to an elderly lady whose main complaint (apart from her aching joints) is that her children and grandchildren don't come to see her as often as they should.

In truth, the doctor only needs to *look* like he's listening. While he may actually just be fantasising about shooting a hole-in-one on the back nine, or giving his receptionist a comprehensive seeing-to, the effect on his patients will be much the same. They say that time is a great healer (though Savlon is recommended for minor cuts and abrasions). So a few minutes of a doctor's time often do more good than a handful of pills. After taking their regular cocktail of tranquillisers, some of his patients forget their own names.

And what happened to Bob? Well, Dr Madeley gave him a tube of ointment, and an inflatable cushion that looked like an outsized donut. He'll have to apply the ointment himself (as Cath keeps reminding him), but the prognosis looks good. In a couple of weeks he'll be as right as... well, as right as rain.

Fun and games

It's games night in the Crown: a weekly event throughout the winter months that gives regulars the chance to display their prowess at darts and dominoes, pool and cards.[1] Old Ted, finding crown green bowling too strenuous these days, is a stalwart of the dominos team. The only time in recent memory that he missed a game was during the floods. And that was only because he couldn't get the outboard motor started. That's how keen he is.

It's strangely reassuring, on a winter's night, to hear the clacking of the pool balls, the riffling of cards and the chinking of glasses. In the background is the random percussion of dominoes being shuffled, laid or knocked on the table – like a friendly poltergeist – whenever a player can't go, with a triumphal flourish as the last tile goes down. If you want to know what's coming up, best check out the fixtures list.[2]

Darts, on the other hand, is a more hazardous affair. You wonder who first had the idea of transferring the noble sport of archery to an indoor setting. Dispensing with longbows, reducing the arrows to a size that can be gripped between thumb and forefinger, and hanging the target on the wall. What a brainwave! And – best of all – encouraging the participants to sup strong beer at the same time. In a sane world, darts players would be isolated in a padded room, where the only people at risk of injury would be each other. Throwing sharpened missiles in a crowded, smokey bar seems like

---

[1] The landlord used to run a regular trivia quiz. But that's all it ever was... trivial. When he made the mistake of asking more challenging questions - like 'Is there a God?' - his customers started complaining of headaches.

[2] Some forthcoming fixtures in the Milltown and District 'Fives & Threes' Dominoes League...
Seers vs Soothsayers (a foregone conclusion, apparently)
Cross-dressers vs Bikers (not for the feint-hearted)
Healers vs Heathens
Witches vs Warlocks
Dealers vs Users (a bit of a needle match, this one)
Shirts vs Skins
(The Pagans have a bye this week)

a recipe for disaster. In any other context, the building would soon be surrounded by armed police, shouting terse instructions through loudhailers.

The Crown has been Ted's local for more than half a century. He's seen more landlords come and go than the Queen has seen prime ministers. But his memory's not what it was, and old habits die hard. He hawks up a throatful of catarrh and expectorates expertly – depositing a ball of phosphorescent phlegm at the exact spot on the carpet where the spittoon would have been, had this been Coronation year.

Even a trip to the urinal is like going into a time capsule – a smelly, unhygienic time capsule that hasn't seen a fresh lick of paint since old Ted's great great grandfather first staggered in to splash his boots. Guys tend to take a deep breath, before opening the door, hoping they'll be back at the bar before they need to take another. Apart from pissing beer up the wall, there are a couple of other reasons for visiting the loo.

There's a tradition at the Crown – though no-one can recall how it started – for drinkers to toss their spare coppers into the trough of the urinal. You could call it a primitive insurance scheme against penury. Imagine this scenario: you're sitting at the bar with an empty glass, a raging thirst and nothing in your pockets except extra strong mints and IOUs. You've run a discreet but probing finger around the lining of your jacket, but found nothing but fluff. What do you do? See if anyone will lend you the price of a pint? Skulk back home and search down the back of the sofa for loose change? No... just nip into the loo, roll up your sleeves, get down on your hands and knees, and scrabble about in the bottom of the urinal, amongst the piss, sputum, fag-ends and those yellow cubes of disinfectant which look (but don't taste...) like pineapple chunks. Scoop up some of those pennies, sluice them under the tap to get rid of the worst of the smell, dry them on your shirt, and, *voila...* you can order another pint of beer *and* retain your dignity.

If you need a drink that badly, good luck to you.

Unless they're broke, the sulphurous atmosphere in the loo encourages few people to linger. Which is a shame, because the graffiti-covered walls are like a history book. A damp, stained, lichen-covered history book that chronicles events both great and small since... well, since somebody first scratched 'Abolish slavery'[3] into the wet plaster.

From the other heartfelt inscriptions you can decipher the preoccupations of the Crown's regulars in the intervening years: 'Repeal the Corn Laws', for example, and 'Relieve Mafeking'. There's a crude observation, of a frankly sexual nature, about Charlotte Brontë, which need not concern us here. There are wartime musings: 'No appeasement, Mr Chamberlain', and 'War... What is it good for?'[4] Among the more recent additions are 'George Davis is innocent'[5], 'Down with mini skirts' and 'Football's coming home'.

Old Ted empties his bladder in a scattergun manner that ensures he always has the urinal to himself. An eyebrow is raised in surprise as he checks out the graffiti. Anne perhaps; Emily at a pinch;

---

[3] Predictably - but depressingly - the Milltown chapter of the Union of Manacle Manufacturers supported the slave masters. "Let's not be too hasty about banning slavery. That's political correctness gone mad! Think of all the jobs that would go if that fool Wilberforce has his way. Think of our comrades in ancillary trades such as chain-making. The Union of Manacle Manufacturers is calling for strike action."

[4] 'Absolutely nothing...'

[5] This was not, incidentally, the same George Davis whose followers dug up the cricket pitch at Headingley in 1975 during the vital, third England vs Australia test match. The graffito refers instead to the George Davis who, in 1896, after a particularly hard winter, was arrested on a charge of stealing a crust of bread. They were difficult times, when a man might be hanged for what might seem to be the most trivial of misdemeanours.

The case was noteworthy more for the manner of Mr Davis' arrest than for the nature of his crime. The police chase was conducted in a leisurely manner, with an appealing sense of fair play. Davis hijacked a barge and set off down the Rochdale Canal in the direction of Manchester. The police gave chase at a brisk walking pace, in their own narrowboat, with its flashing blue oil-lamp. When Davis stopped for lunch at a canal-side tavern, the police kept a respectful distance until he'd drained his glass of mild, and mopped up the last of his mutton stew with his ill-gotten crust... before taking up the chase again. The police eventually made an arrest outside Littleborough, when Davis made an ill-advised stop to take on a shipment of piano legs.

There were psychiatric reports, of course, to determine whether risking his life for just a crust - while leaving the rest of the loaf untouched - could be construed as the actions of a sane man. And then, once the paperwork was in order, George Davis was hanged.

but *Charlotte*? Well... Ted is hazy about history; his memories are gone to the flames, leaving just a fine, white ash behind. He insists he spent two fraught years in the trenches of Pascendale, combatting lice, hunger and rats. Not to mention the Hun. But that was in 1976, by which time the first World War had been over for more than half a century.

The fire is banked up, and the ale flows freely: a fine state of affairs for the regulars, who know that beer is more important than fresh air. Love may make the world go round, if you believe in that sort of guff, but beer makes the world go round and round and round. There's a real ale bus-lane at the bar. The landlord serves lager drinkers when he's good and ready; if they keep waving their glasses at him, he won't serve them at all.

Even beer drinkers can unwittingly offend. "Which beer would you like?", asks the landlord, waving his hand expansively over the handpumps. "Oh, any", says a punter, unwisely, "*It doesn't matter*". It doesn't matter: three words that can shake a real ale drinker to the core, like driving a stake through a vampire's heart. The regulars shuffle along the bar, to disassociate themselves from this heresy. One or two cross themselves. If it doesn't matter what beer you drink, then 99% of the conversation around the bar is rendered meaningless at a stroke.

It can get worse. On the rare occasions that a customer asks for something non-alcoholic, the whole pub goes quiet. For a few seconds the Crown becomes a Bateman cartoon featuring 'The man who walked up to the bar and ordered orange juice'. "I don't drink", he'll say in self-justification: a concept as alien to the guys propping up the bar as sticking needles in their eyes. *I don't drink*: three more words that can stop conversations in mid-flow and turn beer into malt vinegar.

When a man says "I don't drink", what can he possibly mean? That he doesn't socialise? That he can live without any intake of liquids? That he tries to drink... but ends up spilling it? How does he cope with the aching void that alcohol fills so effectively? Just who is he fooling? What kind of man walks into a pub, only to destroy the ambience with such an ostentatious display of austerity? There must be a temperance bar somewhere where a puritan and his hair shirt will feel more at home. At the Crown he'll get a small glass of gloopy juice and pay about £2 for the privilege. He'll be wise not to quibble about the price; people have been thrown out of the pub for less ("You... *out*"... "But why? I don't remember doing anything wrong." "If you can't fucking remember, that just makes it worse. *Out*"). Ripping off a teetotaller restores the mood of conviviality. Honour is satisfied. The hubbub of beery conversation can begin again.

The landlord surveys his grubby little empire with grim satisfaction, as he gives the scotch eggs a light dusting. Hygiene is not a high priority here; a regime of benign neglect gives the Crown an earthy charm. Good pubs don't get to be good by being designed; they get to be good by a process that takes years of drinking, talking amiable bollocks and general wear and tear. It's something that can't just be created on a drawing board, though that doesn't stop people trying. Any fool can make a bar-stool, God knows. But not even the most artful bodger can fake the shiny patina achieved by an overweight man like Ted shifting his weight, from one cheek of his arse to the other, over the course of half a century. Good pubs don't come ready-made, out of a box; good pubs *evolve*.

Renovating pubs is like an expensive game of musical chairs. It goes something like this... The brewery chucks a lot of money at some defeated pub, turning an undistinguished boozer into a theme pub. The locals are told – subtlely but firmly – that their custom is no longer welcome. The doors reopen with a muted fanfare, and, for maybe six months, the pub is *the* place for the young folk to congregate on a Friday night. But they're fickle; their tastes change; they move on to somewhere newer and noisier. There are few things sadder than an empty fun pub whose time has passed. So what do the brewers do? They chuck a lot more money at the place, that's what, hoping that another face-lift will revive its fortunes. Eventually, by a process of elimination, the pub will revert to what it was before all those expensive face-lifts. Except it *won't* be like it was; it will be a fake, a mere pastiche, a joke. Plastic beams are 'exposed'. Walls are painted 'Nicotine' – a colour only made available to the pub trade – to recreate the effect of heavy smoking in a confined space. 'Humorous' slogans, in a phony Yorkshire dialect, are stencilled around the cornices. The beer pumps come from a saleroom and are purely decorative, the beer of choice now being Tetleys Creamflow: a chilled concoction with all the taste and character of a Kleenex tissue. And so it goes. This is not, thankfully, a fate that is likely to befall the Crown, whose comfortably down-at-heel look is totally authentic. Cheers...

Christmas is over for another year (a source of regret only to the criminally insane) and the decorations have been packed away. Within the space of a fortnight, New Year's resolutions have been made, broken and conveniently forgotten. Dumb-bells and rowing machines have been consigned to the box room; the diet books are slid back onto the bookshelf, to join the other works of fiction. What *were* we thinking of?

This is no time for self-denial. In the heart of a Pennine winter, the body craves stodgy comfort food and maybe three months of hibernation. Instead of losing a few pounds, or giving up the weed for good, we just get depressed at our own lack of willpower: a state of mind that's hard to shift, what with the days being so short and dreary. A Pennine winter should be the very opposite of Lent: a time of fervent self-*indulgence*. Yes, that's games night at the Crown: our weekly reaffirmation that life could be worse.

On Heartbreak Hill

It's the last week of February. While optimists may convince themselves that spring is nigh, realists know that winter still has a few tricks to play. Hailstones beat tattoos on our windows; sights and sounds are muffled by flurries of snow. Days of rain have left the ground saturated. Farmers walk sodden fields and, in consequence, fill Dr Madeley's waiting room with pungent agricultural odours and bad cases of trenchfoot.

Not Lester, though. People go to the doctors with a sniffle, and end up with pneumonia. A doctor's waiting room may be fine for idle gossip, but it's no place for people who aren't feeling well. Lester has remedies of his own back at the farm: a tatty old bandage for major lacerations, a shot of whisky for everything else.

Lester's on the tops today, putting a new sheepdog through its paces. His language is the most colourful aspect of a scene overlaid with a cheerless wash of 'Pennine Drizzle' and 'Sleet Grey' – two of the less popular paints from Crown's new 'Depressive' collection. If the darkest hour is just before dawn, then the gloomiest time of year is just before spring erupts with new life and colour and birdsong.

Lester whistles, waves his stick and calls the dog. But he's frustrated, and the name he calls the hapless dog isn't the one that's engraved on its collar ('Prince', the same name as the three other dogs he's had; the same collar too, no point throwing money away). So Prince gets confused, and runs around in circles. Instead of filing meekly into their pen, the sheep scatter like buckshot.

It would be a lot less hassle for Lester if his sheep were cloned, like Dolly. They'd all look much the same, of course, but Lester could live with that. Anyway, it's not like his regular sheep would win prizes for their distinctive personalities. Cloned sheep might at least run in the same damn direction. Lester would have fewer sleepless nights, and spend less time scouring the fells for lost sheep. Every year, at lambing time, there are always a few weaklings that need special attention. Hoisting them over his shoulders – the very image of the Good Shepherd – Lester staggers back to the farmhouse. He's getting too old for all this. The lambs need feeding by hand, with a baby's bottle. Some nights he doesn't get to bed at all. Too old and too tired.

The lambs that survive will soon be back in the fields again, fending for themselves. The lambs that *don't* make it are... well, let's just say that, unlike the Queen Mother, they don't get a state funeral. In the parable the sheep that was lost was worth more than the other ninety nine. That rings a little hollow for a hill farmer like Lester, since all his sheep – lost or found, sound or sickly, dead or alive – are worth about the same when the time comes to auction them at the livestock mart. Fuck all...

Lester's a throwback to another age. He wears a suit – albeit a scruffy one, the kind that scarecrows wear – come rain or shine, and a hat pulled down tight over his ears. He lives alone, farming a hundred unproductive acres high up on Heartbreak Hill. There never seemed to be enough time to get around to marriage, what with so many jobs that needed doing around the farm. In any case, he only ever had one chat-up line: "Would you like to come back to my place and do a little light dusting?" Most young women of marriageable age came to the unarguable conclusion that, no, they probably wouldn't.

To visit Dale Head Farm is like going back fifty years. In fact it's almost *exactly* like going back fifty years; the headline on the yellowed newspaper that doubles as a kitchen tablecloth suggests that time has stood still since the Coronation. Over the years Lester has subjected household chores to a rigorous time and motion study, eventually dispensing with them altogether. What's the point of washing up when you only have to do it all over again *next* month?

The working day (like there was any other kind...) begins early. As he gulps his tea, Lester turns the radio on. The farming programmes used to be worthy but dull: livestock prices, the weather forecast, some patronising guff about not drinking sheep dip on an empty stomach. But those days are gone, and the news from the countryside now seems like a never-ending catalogue of disasters.

The working day ends late. Lester responds to every new farming crisis by working longer and harder. But if a man can't make a half decent living by working *ten* hours a day, is he really going to turn things around by working *twelve*? It doesn't make much sense, but farming's in his blood. Farmers don't go down to the job centre, to see if there might be some other line of work that will suit them better. Farming's not a job, it's a way of life.

That doesn't stop people from giving farmers the benefit of their advice. Diversify, they suggest glibly: convert a barn into a guest house, run a petting zoo, sell premium foods over the internet. But Lester wouldn't know a website from a hole in the ground, and any overnight guests would soon regret not having booked into somewhere more salubrious... like the Bates Motel.

Lester is, in every sense, the last of the line. At one time he regretted not having a son to take over the farm. But not any more. If Lester, with all those years of experience behind him, can't make ends meet, what chance would a greenhorn have? If you are unwise enough to quiz him about the future of hill farming, as he perches morosely on a stool at the far end of the bar, all you will get for your trouble is a torrent of invective and abuse. Yes, anyone who thinks that farmers are slow to show their feelings should see Lester in full flow.

He doesn't suffer fools gladly, or anyone else for that matter. Even those who have taken the time to get to know him often wonder why they bothered. But his place in the affections of Milltown folk is not at the forefront of his mind right now; there are too many other things to worry about. The truth is that Lester was quietly going broke even *before* foot and mouth.

Cows don't milk themselves, so he's been out of the Pennines just once in the last twenty years: to a cousin's wedding in London. "I didn't like the sandwiches", Lester reported later, reducing the rest of humanity to the status of a finger buffet. Despite having been all around the world, Cousin Jack "still hadn't learned that an empty glass needs filling". And "If that's all you learn when you go abroad, then I'd just as soon stay here". Strange, to be so proud of having travelled so little. But a man can't run a farm if he's dreaming of faraway places.

The accountant dreads his annual pilgrimage up to Dale Head Farm almost as much as Lester does. He has to tackle a shoe-box full of grubby receipts that appear to have languished in the back pocket of Lester's trousers for months. He tries to avoid touching anything else, while remembering to refuse every offer of tea. The figures don't add up; they haven't done for years. As he snaps his briefcase shut at the end of the longest day of his financial year, he offers a few words of advice. Lester knows what's coming; he's heard it all before. "I've done your books as best I can, Lester, but I'd be neglecting my duty as a friend..." (there's an arm around Lester's shoulder at this point in the familiar homily) "...if I didn't point out that the only sensible way forward would be to sell up, bank the money and spend the rest of your days sunning yourself on the beaches of the Costa del Sol." "Same time next year, then?", says Lester, as he holds the door open.

He doesn't need to work on his tan, in Andalucia or anywhere else. It's hard to imagine him straying far from Heartbreak Hill. It's even harder to see him retiring. What the hell does a retired farmer do with his time? Dig an allotment? Collect first day covers? Sit in the old folks' home, while some bearded loon with a guitar tries to get a bunch of incontinent codgers to join in the chorus of 'Old MacDonald had a farm'? The very thought makes him shudder.

Lester will carry on farming until he himself is planted in good

Pennine earth. What will become of Dale Head Farm when he's gone? Well, it could be transformed into a weekend cottage for a commodities broker from Leeds or Manchester. With a few additions of no architectural merit it could be the clubhouse of yet another golf course. It could fall down stone by stone, slate by slate, year by year – to join the other hill farms around Milltown that are quietly going back to nature. If it's still a working farm in ten years time, then we'll know that miracles *do* happen.

Dog day afternoon

Things had been going pretty well for Rob and Sue. They'd weathered the first, heady days of their relationship, and even their more sceptical friends conceded they made a good-looking couple. Sue seemed the responsible one, a wise head on young shoulders. But once Rob had revised his rather immature definition of the perfect partner (an infatuated orphan who, despite being a home-loving virgin, has somehow mastered the art of sucking a golf-ball through fifty feet of garden hose), he too felt ready for a degree of commitment.

When Sue suggested they move in together, Rob was all ears. Two could live as cheaply as one, she insisted. The conversation was pretty one-sided. Rob's cramped bedsit was no place for a young couple; even a couple of cockroaches might have had second thoughts. No-one visited his room unless they wanted to read the meter: the stench of Brut, body odour and Biactol was overpowering. There was a greasy, grey-green Galapagos beneath the bathtub, where plants that shunned light could quietly thrive. His bed-sheets were crisp, like poppadums. And at the back of Rob's fridge something was throbbing: something he preferred to leave alone. A change of scenery couldn't have come at a better time.

Rob moved into Sue's airy flat with a heady mixture of excitement and apprehension. It looked so perfect: a place for everything, and everything in its place. Some days, while Sue was out at work, he would creep around the flat on tiptoes. His natural curiosity vied with the uncomfortable feeling that he was trespassing. The first time the doorbell rang, Rob jumped two feet in the air. His first reaction was to hide behind the sofa, until he remembered he lived here too.

He tried, without success, to pick the lock of her five-year diary. He stood in front of her bedroom mirror with an imaginary guitar, entertaining an unseen audience with his full repertoire of guitar god poses. Investigating Sue's knicker drawer, he found a small bundle of love letters tied up with a blue ribbon. At least he *assumed* they were love letters. If a man were to keep love letters, they would be in a filing cabinet, filed under 'L' (not for 'Love', of course, but for 'Letters') along with his utility bills and cheque book stubs. Rob slid Sue's letters back, unread, amongst her frilly briefs, but not before he'd tried a pair on. You'd do the same, you know you would.

Sue had a mug tree, a Toilet Duck and the full set of Stain Devils. Even the loo seat seemed to be giving him a subliminal message; it wouldn't stay up on its own. Rob kept it up with one knee, which didn't improve his aim. As he sniffed the air freshener and furniture polish, Rob had his first misgivings. Surrounded by spice racks and nick-nacks, he felt surplus to requirements, out of place... like the guy in the Corrs.

A proper grown-up relationship represented a steep learning curve for a naive young guy of twenty who'd left school four years earlier with some glaring gaps in his portfolio of social skills. While girls play with dolls and develop their nurturing potential, boys run around the playground with pretend pump-action rifles, shouting *"Ack-ack-ack-ack... you're dead"*. No prizes for guessing which sex is better equipped to foster meaningful attachments.

Rob's education really only started *after* he'd left school. He ticked off, one by one, the milestones in a young man's rite of passage into the adult world. He rode a motorbike. He drank strong cider. He slept with a woman. He slept with a woman who wasn't drunk. He slept with a woman who wasn't drunk, without money changing hands. There was nothing wrong with the lad; if it was quiet you could actually hear his hormones humming.

He thought he knew about women but then, at sixteen, he thought he knew everything. After a few beers, he immortalised his first girlfriend by having 'Janice 4 Ever' tattooed on his arm. That timescale proved optimistic; two weeks later she'd found a guy with a car, and had given Rob the elbow. Chastened by the experience, Rob had the incriminating tattoo incorporated into a more elaborate design – the *Raft of the Medusa*, after Géricault – which cost him two weeks wages and quite a few sleepless nights.

If a woman patted his belly, in a friendly kind of way, and suggested he'd "put on a pound or two", Rob learned that this didn't give him the right to do the same to *her*. He learned to read between the lines of what women say. "No" meant "*no*"; after a few false starts he managed to get that straight. But there were still some baffling euphemisms to interpret. If a woman said she'd got the painters in, that meant he'd be taking the last bus home. But if she said she had the *builders* in, that just meant she had the builders in. As long as he could pick his way through the rubble, and didn't mind brick-dust in his cocoa, he could book himself in for bed and breakfast.

He wondered what women meant, exactly, when they finished a relationship with the hope that "we can still be friends"? What... they'd be happy to go round car-breakers' yards with him, looking for a transmission for a late-model Ford Capri? What... they'd come on a pub-crawl with him, talk about football, sex and cars, and drink strong lager to the point of unconsciousness? What *could* these women mean?

His education continued apace. He discovered that a letter beginning 'You may already be a winner' is not necessarily a life-changing event. He learned, to his chagrin, that pro wrestling is rigged, and that prostitutes don't really look like the pictures on their cards. Even his first water bill came as a shock. No-one had informed Rob that he'd have to pay for something that fell out of the South Pennine skies with such depressing regularity.

Once he'd moved into Sue's flat, the poor sap was pathetically eager to please. He tackled the washing up, thinking this would give him control of the TV remote on Saturday evenings and the right to watch an uninterrupted diet of football, footballing interviews and other football-related punditry. He was wrong. Rob made the ultimate sacrifice: instead of playing five-a-side football with his mates one Saturday morning, he accompanied Sue to the supermarket. He imagined this selfless act would earn him some Brownie points. He was wrong about that too. All he'd done was to establish a precedent for every Saturday morning until the end of time.

Rob and Sue spent what was left of their weekends looking round Barratt show-homes. As well as checking out the soft furnishings, Sue took this as an opportunity to discuss their relationship. She talked about getting married and settling down: another concept that Rob needed explaining. 'Getting married' seemed simple enough; it was what your parents did. But 'settling down': surely that's what happened to a box of cornflakes in transit. Tagged onto the end of 'getting married and settling down' was the unspoken rider: '...instead of whooping it up and having fun'. This wasn't a door opening to new possibilities, it felt like a door slamming shut.

As one of those young women who relish a challenge, Sue felt duty bound to knock off some of Rob's rougher edges. His naivety, though quite attractive at first, was wearing thin. Rob got the vague feeling that he was being worked on, like a school project: a feeling that wasn't dispelled by Sue pinning his mittens to the sleeves of his jacket. Men like to be loved, cherished even. But they don't like to be fussed over. And, yes, whisper it, Sue is a bit of a fuss-pot.

The time had come for Rob to meet Sue's folks: a daunting prospect. He borrowed a shirt and tie for the occasion. It wasn't that he kicked against the dictates of fashion; fashion was just one more concept that passed him by altogether, like quantum physics or Heisenberg's Principle of Uncertainty.

With a good excuse to buy herself a new dress, Sue dragged Rob around the shops. "What do you think?", she said, giving him a twirl. "Be honest." But the language of diplomacy was not one that Rob spoke with any fluency. "You look great" would have been a good start, while waiting for the appropriate adjectives to form an orderly queue in his mind. But Rob, in a doomed attempt to find the right words, waited a nano-second too long. "You don't like the dress", said Sue, flatly, pulling the changing room curtains closed again – thus instigating another three hours of shopping.

Sue made reassuring noises – "You'll be fine" – as she parked the car outside a smart terraced house with a panoramic view of Milltown. She spat on her handkerchief, absent-mindedly, and wiped an imaginary speck of dirt from Rob's cheek. "Mum and dad are really looking forward to meeting you". And so they were. Sue's dad ("Call me Arthur") pumped his hand enthusiastically. Mum Barbara, a fragrant cloud of eau de cologne, offered her cheek for Rob to peck. A younger sister, Yvonne, was disturbingly, head-turningly pretty. There was a bloke who smoked a pipe (an uncle?) and a couple of garrulous ladies who chattered in unison, like parrots. What... giddy aunts?

Everyone was so friendly, but Rob still felt out of place and under scrutiny. He ran a finger under his shirt collar, to stop it choking him. He half expected the family to hold up cards, like they do in ice-skating, to judge his performance. He hoped he'd pass muster – for technical merit, if not artistic impression – but he wouldn't put folding money on it. While he was under their roof, Rob had to pretend that the most intimate thing he and Sue got up to was to hold hands and read Proust aloud to each other. It was all a bit of a strain for the lad.

The house was immaculate, like a National Trust gift shop. There was quilted toilet paper in the loo; for a guy who'd spent years recycling old newspapers it was like walking barefoot on shagpile carpet. The bookcase was full of titles published by the AA and Readers Digest. *The AA Book of Celebrity Breakfasts. The Big Bumper Book of Scottish Cuisine. The Beginner's Guide to Collecting Broken Biscuits.* Rob had often wondered who bought this kind of stuff, and now he knew. Whenever he was tempted to put his teacup down on a polished tabletop, Barbara was hovering close by with a doyley. He could see where Sue got her more fastidious habits from. A lot of things began to fall into place, and not in a good way.

They were a close-knit family – so close that they communicated in a kind of verbal shorthand. Sentences were left unfinished, their understanding seemed telepathic. They told jokes so old and familiar that they'd obviously become family heirlooms. Sometimes all they needed to say were the punchlines ("...But it wasn't my bike!"... "...Who *said* I was drilling for oil?..." "...Well, the *pig* never complained!...") and everyone fell about laughing. What reinforced the family bond only made Rob feel more of an outsider. "Make yourself at home", Sue's mother said, with a smile, but he felt like he was visiting another planet. These people weren't a family, they were a *cult*. Nobody hugged when *his* family got together, they just exchanged business cards. And the only family tradition *he* could recall was farting in alphabetic order.

The highlight of the visit was Sunday lunch, the dramatic set-piece of a fly-on-the-wall documentary with a working title of 'Sue's Family'. Sue played footsie with Rob under the table, in a noble attempt to keep his spirits up. Barbara piled his plate with roast beef, boiled potatoes and vegetables. As they raised their glasses in a toast ("The Queen", said Arthur, with no detectable irony) Rob remembered his instructions, and avoided any reference to sodomy, New Labour, their daughter's sexual proclivities, and any other contentious topics of conversation.

Inevitably, under the influence of a schooner of sweet sherry, he began to relax a little. So when a potato went AWOL – slipping off his fork and into his lap – he launched confidently into a simple diversionary tactic. "Look", he said, suddenly inspired. "Look out of the window everyone". Heads turned, following his pointed finger, as Rob slipped the potato back onto his plate. That went well, he thought, until he too glanced out of the window. There, on the tiny lawn, two of the neighbours' dogs were shagging each other senseless.

That was two months ago. Arthur offered a financial inducement for Rob never to see his daughter again ("Did we really fight two World Wars for the right to watch dogs mating?"). It would have been a needless expense, since Sue was quite capable of taking her own revenge. Overnight that sweet-tempered lass turned into Lady Macbeth. She tore up the holiday photos and shredded Rob's favourite jeans. After she'd removed his number from the speed-dialler on her mobile phone, she did things to his stereo with a tub of custard-style yoghurt that instantly invalidated the manufacturer's warranty.

Sue's friends rallied round. "We never liked Rob", they said, in a misguided attempt to cheer her up. "You're better off without him." At the very moment that Sue needed a listening ear, all she got was fatuous advice.

For someone who said she wasn't speaking to Rob, Sue seemed to have a great deal to say. She delivered her well-practiced speech and, with a note of finality, handed him two bin-bags full of his clothes, CDs, trainers and Odour Eaters. "One day", she told Rob, coldly, "you may wish you hadn't always shied away from commitment". But Rob isn't *shying* away from commitment... he's *running* away, as fast as his legs can carry him.

It's back to school for Rob. He replays the relationship like a video, freeze-framing significant moments to try and see where it started to go downhill. Then he switches over to the football. He's almost convinced himself that he's better off without Sue. It's the price of growing up that no-one sorts things out when they go wrong. There's no-one to kiss his grazed elbow better, and he has to be a contortionist to do it himself. The safety net has been taken down; he's on his own.

Now, freed from the claustrophobic confines of coupledom, Rob can do whatever he wants, whenever it suits him. He can do the washing up tomorrow, or leave it until next week. He can wear odd socks, neglect his personal hygiene and fart at will. He can keep the toilet seat up all the time; and if he can't be bothered to climb the stairs, he can just piss in the sink. He can go to the cinema on his own, eat Pot Noodles instead of proper meals... and drink cans of Special Brew to try and numb the pain.

Ravages of time

Shops come and go in Milltown. They open up like spring flowers, to meet our real or imaginary needs for organic cheeses, ethnic handicrafts and occult paraphernalia. Some of them disappear even before we realise they've opened. When people decide to "do without advertising and just see how it goes", we know for certain that their trading days are numbered. Let's be straight on the matter: starting a business without advertising is like shouting in a whisper.

Drip-dry wedding dresses were never going to be hot selling items in a place like Milltown. And 'Wicca World': what the hell was *that* all about? The record for sinking without trace is currently held by a second-hand shop selling Indian clothing. 'Whose Sari Now?' proved to be a rhetorical question. The boutique opened on a Friday and had closed by the Monday, without even adding to the £20 float.

But still they come: retailing rookies with exotic ideas, family windfalls and the optimism of the damned, ready to give shopkeeping a whirl. To counteract the gravitational pull of the out-of-town supermarkets, it might be more profitable to target the old, the infirm and those who've had their cars repossessed: the kind of people who *have* to shop locally. Offer 'Everything for a Quid', with some appropriate background Musak ('Buddy, can you spare a dime?'... 'Nobody loves you when you're down and out'), and wait for the money to roll in. The entrepreneurs of Milltown tend to have more exotic ideas, however, spotting niche markets so small that they're almost invisible to the naked eye. One short-lived shop made a brief speciality out of *im*practical jokes, but who – beyond the small and shadowy world of S & M – buys exploding suppositories?

Like some tragic hero on the operatic stage, other shops are a long time dying. Their closing down sales stretch out to weeks, months, even years. Sometimes those 'Sale Must End On Saturday' posters get so tatty they have to be replaced with new ones. And perhaps someone could explain to us why a florist needs to have a closing down sale at all.

So we're watching with more than usual interest as yet another emporium prepares to open up. Who knows, maybe someone will finally get their sums right. Jude reads the name over the door. Zimmer Man. It seems vaguely familiar. Pressing his nose up against the window pane, he finds a disconcerting display of stuff for old folk. Nothing they might actually *want* (like cream sherry or shortbread biscuits or butterscotch) but what they apparently *need*. Stannah stairlifts, artfully disguised commodes, telescopic walking sticks, reclining chairs, adjustable beds, zimmer frames and electric shopping buggies. These are the tools of the trade for ageing hippies: polished chrome and leatherette, with some flesh-coloured plastic thrown in for good measure.

It's all quite a shock to Jude's system: an unwelcome reminder of his own mortality. It's way too late for him to die young and pretty, and – despite what he thought at seventeen – he isn't going to live for ever. At seventeen life stretched out ahead, like a mirage: a tantalising dream of endless promise. Nothing seemed impossible.

It all seems so very long ago. Michael Jackson was black, the trains ran on time, and when we had a war the other side fought back; yes, *that's* how long ago it was. The first storm clouds gathered over the Summer of Love, to usher in the Autumn of Disillusionment. One-man buses, televised snooker, one-day cricket, Vesta packet meals... what *was* the world coming to?

But now Jude's in his fifties – an indeterminate time of life with very little to recommend it. He can't even use his age as one of the lottery numbers any more. People talk about being 'only thirty' as in "I'm only thirty... still plenty of time to start a family". And "I'm only forty... still plenty of time for a change of career". But what follows 'only fifty'? "I'm only fifty... still time to book an appointment with the proctologist"? "Still time to become a storm-trooper for Age Concern"? "Still time to take up crown green bowling"? *Fifty?* Fuck it...

Jude has to face up to the prospect of old age, however unpleasant it may be. As the tail-lights of the twentieth century retreat into the gloom, Jude has a glimpse of the future. It doesn't look good. Meals on wheels. Sitting in a rocking chair, too tired even to get it going. Huddling over a one-bar electric fire, indulging in an orgy of bitterness, recrimination and regret. Watching snuff movies that have snuff in them. Trying to roll a joint with arthritic fingers, then having to wait for the District Nurse to call round and put the roach in. And, worst of all, the prospect of spending his declining years in the old folks' home (Sunset House: 'Serving the decrepit and incontinent since 1985'). Jude gives an involuntary shudder. He doesn't want to end his days like his grandad: just sitting around the house all day, waiting for TV to be invented.

Yes, if the superannuated hippies of Milltown had known they were going to live *this* long, they might have taken rather better care of themselves. Jude, for one, smoked heavily throughout his youth, mostly to collect the coupons. His heart was set on a touring caravan, but his lungs had other ideas. By the time his favourite brand had been withdrawn (for being so high in tar you could have mended the roads with it) he'd accumulated only enough coupons for a workshop manual and a set of adjustable spanners.

He might have been a little more selective about his drug intake too. But, like so many others of his generation, Jude reckoned that being doped up to the eyeballs was a job only half done. He laboured under the misapprehension that by dropping acid he was helping to destroy the system (the system, no; his *nervous* system, yes). The police used to arrest stoned hippies on sight[1], only

---

[1] West Yorkshire Police urged youngsters to "Get hooked on fishing, not drugs and crime". Meanwhile, the Union of Dace, Chub and other Freshwater Fish had a rather different message: "Don't be too hasty about that. Don't discount the many pleasures that drugs and crime have to offer".

adopting a more pragmatic 'watching brief' when they realised they couldn't arrest *everyone* in Milltown. Someone had to keep those vital services going.

At the summer festivals, Jude might not have stood quite so close to the sound system. There's a constant, angry buzzing in his head these days, like a wasp in a jar. As he's now painfully aware, dancing around a muddy field, with flowers in his hair, did not make him immune to the twin terrors of age and gravity. "Hope I die before I get old" Roger Daltrey sang way back in 1965. But you don't hear him singing *that* any more, do you? Oh no. It's all trout farms and American Express now. Bastard

Sunset House was purpose-built as a 'drive-thru' establishment – allowing successful people with busy lives to abandon their elderly hippy relatives with a minimum of fuss, paperwork or sentiment. And, with Sunset House operating a 'no questions asked' policy, a lot of old folk arrive under cover of darkness. It's an all too familiar scenario. A car, its headlights off, cruises down the drive, as quietly as possible. But that's not so easy on gravel.

In the dormitories of Sunset House, light sleepers awake. If they gnaw through their straps, and peer through the windows, residents will see – or, more likely, just hear – what's happening in the courtyard below. The car stops, the passenger door opens. There's a dull thud, perhaps a yelp of pain, and the car door slams shut again. Fuelled by relief and guilt – always a combustible mixture – the driver throws caution to the wind. Gunning the car through the gears – spinning tyres, scattering gravel, waiting till he reaches the end of the drive to switch the headlights on – he's away down the road towards a new life, free from the shackles of responsibility.

Next morning the residents will find their number increased by one: some disorientated old duffer, with nothing except the clothes he's stood up in, a Crackerjack pen & pencil set and a scrunched-up note in his fist that reads: 'Hello. My name is Jack. Blood type O. Tea, not coffee. Honey Nut Loops. I talk to myself. Thank you'.

One by one, the old hippies of Milltown are winding up at Sunset House. Some go willingly enough, won over by promises of Sunny Delight for breakfast – the tartrazine gets them kick-started on a morning – and that heady Horlicks rush at the end of the day. The staff do their best to keep the residents' minds active ("Let's try it again, Mr Skynyrd. Look: arse... elbow... No, no... *Arse... elbow...*") but it's not easy.

A one-way ticket on a Sixties-bound Tardis; who could pass up an offer like that? Set the controls for the Summer of Love. Whizz straight past the Seventies, the decade that died of shame... but be sure to stop well short of the Fifties, that gloomy time of rationing and Brylcreem when everyone lived in black & white.

Ah, yes, the Sixties... What a great time to be young, optimistic and in full control over vital sphincter muscles. A golden age when men were fermenting revolution and women were making coffee. Simpler times when we had farthings, florins, fahrenheit and fuzzy felt. Antirrhinums, antimacassars and avoidupois. Dubbin and dolly blue. Green Shield stamps, twin-tubs, tiger nuts, spanish, singing cowboys, coltsfoot rock, barley sugar twists, temperance hotels, sarsaparilla, sweet cigarettes (what a great idea *they* were: introducing kids to a lifetime of addiction to sugar *and* nicotine), ginger beer, lemon curd, lead soldiers, penny plain and tuppence coloured.

We could leave our front doors unlocked back then, without any bother. We'd keep the doors wide open, all through the night. When we went on holiday we'd leave notes for the burglars, telling them the house would be empty for a fortnight. We left explicit instructions about where they could find the valuables. Sometimes we'd even go so far as to put a small ad in the local paper. But did we ever get burgled? Did we buggery...

Ah, the Sixties... that semi-mythical time when unicorns roamed the earth, Concorde was the future of travel, and, thanks to Neil Armstrong's "Giant step for Mankind", we got non-stick frying pans and pens that could write upside-down. Tell *that* to anyone who says the space race was just a huge waste of money.

People knew their neighbours back then; people knew their place; the summers were warm, the winters were cold, like seasons *should* be; kids respected their elders; for a fair day's work you got a fair day's pay; you could walk the streets without getting mugged for your mobile, and AIDS was an ineffectual slimming product rather than a global plague of terrifying proportions. Waggon Wheels were so big back then that they wouldn't even fit into your satchel; you had to bowl them back from the shop like hoops. Now look at them. Pitiful. Yes, if the past is, indeed, another country, the old folk of Milltown would have few complaints at being repatriated.

That's the great thing about nostalgia. Being an essentially meaningless concept, the Golden Age can be any time in the past: Ancient Greece, the Rennaisance, the 1960s, a week last Wednesday. Memory Lane has probably been upgraded to an eight-lane motorway by now. It really doesn't matter.

There are some old hippies, though, who have no need to go back to the Sixties... for the simple reason that they never really left. After a lifetime of half-arsed anarchy and solvent abuse, these grizzled old graybeards have no intention of going gentle into that good night... or into the claustrophobic confines of Sunset House either. They've managed thus far to avoid the Poll Tax, meaningful labour and the preoccupations of the *petit bourgeoisie*, so it's going to take more than a packet of Old English Spangles to persuade *them* to sit in a reclining chair, staring catatonically at the point where the wall meets the ceiling.

They take some rounding up, these old guys, once they've gone native. The best time to catch them is after a few pipefuls of home grown, when their defences are down and they've got the munchies. The strategy: tempt them to follow a trail of Pringles into what is still the only council-operated man-trap in the county.

Once inside, even the wildest child of the Sixties can be sedated with Furry Freak Brothers cartoons or a dose of Incredible String Band (not the difficult third album, of course, which is more likely to enrage them). The last resort – and one that Sunset House is loathe to publicise – is to call out the local vet. As defiant as these old guys may sound ("You'll never take me alive... I can remember when this was all fields") they've no answer to a tranquilliser dart.

Jude arrived in Milltown at the spliff-end of the Sixties, with a guitar slung over his shoulder and a repertoire of protest songs. He came here for all the usual reasons: to escape from his creditors, keep his head down and find a ready supply of recreational drugs. Back then he was a pillar of the anti-establishment. He laughed in the face of convention; he spat in the eye of normality. Like everyone else at the time, he wanted to overthrown capitalism, fight for the rights of the working man, and get laid (but not necessarily in that order). He manned barricades, shouted slogans and broke innumerable by-laws – except, of course, on Giro day.

He organised a sit-down protest against the war in Vietnam. At a pre-arranged signal, two dozen people sat down in the road. They brought traffic to a standstill for, oh, about five minutes, until drivers found they could make a small detour. The protesters sat and sat, waiting for the police to come and arrest them. When the police eventually showed up – a Panda car made a brief recce – they took one look at this raggle-taggle army and began to walk back to their car. "Aren't you going to arrest us, you copper bastards?", said Jude. "I don't think that will be necessary", said the first PC, holding out his hand, palm upwards, and glancing up at the sky. He was right, of course. A few minutes later the heavens opened, and one by one the soggy protesters went home.

Typical: when you need a copper to arrest you in a righteous cause, read you your rights and then drag you kicking and screaming into the back of a black maria... they're nowhere to be seen. But if you just happen to 'liberate' a couple of frozen chickens from the Co-op – a victimless crime if there ever was one – the pigs are onto you straight away.

It wasn't the cause he would have chosen, but what the hell. When asked to grass up his co-conspirators, Jude stood firm. He acted alone, he said. The frozen chickens were for his own personal use. The police gave him a Chinese burn. It really hurt. Jude reconsidered his options. He was prepared to divulge the age and sexual predilections of his accomplices, even their inside leg measurements. But their names? Never! The police would have to torture him first. The police tortured him. Jude suggested he might provide just his co-conspirators' first names and maybe an initial. The police tortured him some more. He squealed like a girl, begged for mercy and said he was prepared to tell them everything they wanted to know... and quite a lot besides (including all the winners of the FA Cup since 1904).

One year Jude stood for the council, on an Anarcho-Syndicalist platform. He urged his supporters, such as they were, to boycott the election. It was "an imperialist sham", he insisted. So convincing was his rhetoric, and so righteous was his cause, that he gathered no votes at all (having been too busy on polling day to vote himself). It was merely the first of a long list of pointless gestures. Jude went on hunger strike to protest about the violation of human rights in the third world – only to change his mind when he fully comprehended what happens to people who don't eat. On another occasion he was tricked into giving up a silent vigil, when a policeman handed him his walkie-talkie and said "Hey, Che Guevara... it's for you."

The Beatles split up, which had a disorientating effect on Jude, and prevented him making plans further ahead than lunchtime. That year, 1970, marked the beginning of his withdrawal from reality, and into a kind of fantasy world of his own invention. Fortunately, a lot of Milltown folk were already living there too, so he was seldom short of company. Is cannabis addictive? Jude never stopped smoking long enough to find out. Drink, drugs and promiscuous sex were an everyday aspect of Milltown life back then; even the invitations to children's parties read 'Bring Bottle and Bird'.

There followed a period about which Jude has no recollection at all – mostly due to ingesting enough class A drugs to fell a herd of elephants. When he wasn't able to work, it was "because of the drink and the drugs". While some misguided souls might see this as a ringing endorsement of drink and drugs, Jude now wonders what he might have achieved in life if he hadn't taken a stoned lemming as his role model. He staggered through the Doors of Perception – in search of new and intriguing addictions – only to get hopelessly lost in the Vestibule of Tedium and the Inner Sanctum of Utter Incomprehensibility. The doors of perception proved to be *revolving* doors. For three whole years Jude was convinced he was a satsuma.

Though his life was in freefall, Jude felt powerless to change. He saw the world in simplistic terms: just big shapes and loud noises. To anyone who has had to cope with the wiles and ways of an addict, the scenario will be depressingly familiar: the dabbling, the bluster, the bravado, the impotence, the pain, the self-loathing, the descent into hell, the resolutions, the good intentions, the false starts, the stark realisations, the long road to recovery, the convalescence, the sheer mind-numbing boredom, the 'addict in recovery' gibbering (which could clear a crowded lift in seconds). "I am a member of a drug survival programme", Jude would mumble at every opportunity, "and I would like to read you a poem".

It wasn't the love of a good woman that finally pulled Jude through. There had been a few women in his life, some of them good-hearted, but none of them had wanted to dedicate their lives selflessly to a drug-addled loser like Jude. At some point in the relationship they would give him an ultimatum – "You're going to have to choose: it's either the drugs or me" – and that would be that. No, what revitalised Jude was getting back into his music. He called up four of his old buddies for a jam session. By the time they'd busked some songs and sunk a few beers, they'd become a band: The Uncles.

Success didn't come easily for The Uncles. Or, indeed, at all.[2] They were so bad that they could play in pubs that don't even have an entertainment licence. They would try to *start* each song together, and finish together; but what happened in between was in the lap of the gods. They battled against all odds, refusing to be cowed by the world's indifference. By dint of endless touring – as far afield as, oh, Mytholmroyd and Bacup – they went on to become the premier soft-rock outfit in the valley. You remember them, of course you do: the duelling kazoos, those five-part harmonies and the extended drum solos that sounded like two dozen dustbins being hurled down a spiral staircase. They even put out a thousand copies of what turned out to be their one and only CD: The Uncles, Unhinged.

Instead of the mundane realities of life in a small, South Pennine milltown, their music reflected a romantic affinity for rural Americana. The Uncles didn't get their kicks on the A646 (a road that was noteworthy only for being dug up every few weeks) but on Route 66. When they went down to the crossroads, they weren't thinking about the one in Milltown, where old biddies in carpet slippers would wander absent-mindedly into the traffic.

All things must pass, however, and The Uncles split up in the middle of their annual farewell reunion concert: an event that was in any case suffering from the law of diminishing returns. The official line was 'musical differences', a tactful way of saying that for most

---

[2] But the Uncles came close... In 1975 Jude penned a song, dedicated to the bass-player's wife, who was known for her luxuriant growth of pubic hair. While some women trimmed their bush into, say, the shape of a heart, she was able to recreate the chariot race from Ben Hur.

'Shave Your Missus for Me' was Jude's melodic response. But instead of being the first single of a lucrative career, the tune was hijacked by an unscrupulous music publisher, who changed the lyrics. Brotherhood of Man drew away the competition at the 1976 Eurovision Song Contest, and took their bastardised version - 'Save Your Kisses for Me' - to the top of the charts. The rest is history.

of the time they were playing different songs. But, in truth, the guys in the band were ready to leave the moment they first heard Jude refer to them as "the guys in the band". He seemed to think he was the one indispensable member, just because he owned the van. Then the drummer started getting ideas above his station. "When do we get to play *my* songs?", he would whine, echoing Ringo's words, all those years ago.

The last straw came when an ageing groupie wrinkled up her nose at Jude, and put her top back on. "I'll do anything for love", she said, "but I won't do *that*" – proving not merely that the band's appeal was waning, but also that there are few moments in life that can't be summed up succinctly by the lyric from a Meatloaf song.

Jude was tired of cranking out the same old songs, to a small and increasingly apathetic audience, while tribute bands were pulling in the crowds. Why bother creating new music when it was easier just to hang onto the coat-tails of the famous? Yes, you could see a different tribute band just about every night of the week in Milltown. Poxy Music: a creditable attempt to resuscitate the ailing Spandex industry. Punk Floyd: giving a novel, thrash-metal twist to the back catalogue of the ponderous pomp-rockers. The *Global* Village People: hard to categorise, impossible to listen to. Bloody Holly and the Crickets: like Marilyn Manson, but with National Health spectacles. Gruesome. The Litter Band: trying to kick-start a glam-rock revival in the face of almost universal revulsion.

❖ ❖ ❖

In the good old days our rock star heroes had the sense to die of drink and drugs, allowing us to remember them as they were in their prime. Jimi Hendrix isn't touring the scampi 'n' chips supper-club circuit, thank God, with a 'Hits of the Sixties' nostalgia package. No, Jimi's star never had the chance to wane. He lives on in our memories – still lighting up the night sky at Woodstock with his incandescent licks.

John Lennon's still sitting at that famous white piano. "Imagine no possessions", he sings plaintively, "I wonder if you can". *He* can't, to be frank, but maybe *you* can. Everyone remembers where they were when John Lennon was shot. Jude was watching TV at the time, unless he was out shopping.

Sid Vicious is still doing to *My Way* what the Japanese did to Pearl Harbour, and sharing life, love and dirty needles at the Chelsea Hotel with the lovely Nancy. If we feel for anyone in their sorry tale of rock excess, it's those who are left behind to pick up the pieces. Respect, then, to Mr and Mrs Vicious in their sad loss, and, indeed, to the whole Vicious family.

Janis Joplin never got the chance to be a Peace Ambassador for the United Nations and make a prat of herself all over Africa ("I can understand how these famine victims must feel", she never got the chance to say. "*I* skip lunch too. You have to if you want to keep your figure and stay ahead in the music business"). Janis crawled into a bottle, instead, and never came out.

Elvis had the right idea – only his timing was out by about ten years. Instead of hitting the Las Vegas come-back trail, to become the first of a million Elvis Presley impersonators, he should have quit while he was ahead. We could remember him as he was in 1963, sexy and snake-hipped, not as the fatso who, during a session of colonic irrigation to dislodge almost two stone of impacted faeces from his lower bowel, exploded with a bang that reverberated throughout the state of Tenessee.

Despite all the odds, and their best efforts to kill themselves, some stars have survived. Keith Richards, for example, has been road-testing pharmaceutical products on behalf of a grateful nation (like a beagle offering to buy his own fags) yet *he's* still around. Chris de Burgh hasn't been shot by a crazed fan, though we haven't given up hope altogether. And then there's Ringo. He wasn't the best drummer in the world. He wasn't even the best drummer in the Beatles. But, by golly, he could pick his friends. What next for the once-legendary percussionist and Thomas the Tank Engine narrator: Dictionary Corner on Countdown, perhaps, exchanging doomed pleasantries with Richard Whiteley and accepting his appearance fee in groceries ("Not the drinks department, though. Sorry, Mr Starr").

Gary Glitter elevated self-parody to an artform, but now his features look course and raddled – the wig a sad mockery, the arched eyebrows no longer quizzical but cynical. He's been airbrushed out of musical history, thank goodness, like Stalin from the Politburo. There'll be no more comebacks for the comeback king.

Even before his downfall, Jonathan King was a benchmark for all that was tawdry and trivial in popular music. "You can't send *me* to prison. I'm a celebrity. I've been on TV, for God's sake, I've had my own show". Jim Morrison wrote 'Strange Days' and died in a hot bath; Jonathan King wrote 'Leap up and down and wave your knickers in the air', and will probably live to be a hundred. There's no justice.

✧ ✧ ✧

Jude is fifty four, exactly twice the age that Jim, Janis and Jimi were when they died. Spooky. By the age of twenty seven, Alexander the Great had conquered the known world. In contrast, by the age of twenty seven Jude had mastered the first few chords of Stairway to Heaven. It's always hard to realise that it's probably too late to make much of a stir in this world. The great work may remain undone, the expansive gesture left unmade. But Jude's not ready to hang up his rock 'n' roll shoes just yet. He's not going to wait for the boney finger of Old Father Time to come knocking on his door. He knows his hell-raising days are over. Even burning the candle at *one* end seems beyond him now. And he's given up the dope too. After all, why would any self-respecting anarchist want to smoke cannabis, now that even Tory MPs are pressing for legalisation?

Ten years after they broke up, Jude has reformed The Uncles.

There were a few ruffled feathers to smooth down, a few egos to massage. The clincher, though, was the need to fund three ugly and expensive divorces. The easiest thing would have been to live off past glories, belting out the old favourites with maybe a new twist (We're All Going on a Saga Holiday... Hit Me With Your Walking Stick... When I Was 64...), but Jude and the boys (*boys?*) have other plans. They've decided to go with the flow, instead, and become their very own tribute band. The Carbuncles are on stage tonight in Milltown. Ten years is a long time to be away from the big time; will anyone turn up? Let's hope there's a good crowd. Everyone needs a bit of luck. For inspiration, Jude thought back to Elvis's manager. After all, until Elvis came along, his most marketable act was Colonel Parker's Dancing Chickens.

Jude wangled a 20% discount on his zimmer frame: it would give the shop some free publicity, he said. It stops him falling over when he reaches for the mike. "It's good to be wherever we are", he announces, to the darkened room, "and if we've been here before then it's good to be back"...

Highdays and holidays

There are places people want to visit at holiday times... and places people are glad to get away from. There's no doubt about where we stand in the scheme of things: the prospect of a lazy afternoon in Milltown, celebrating the less-than-rivetting fact that the banks are shut, can summon the scum of five counties. Yes, like swallows – but bigger, and with wallets – the visitors are back.

The world and his common law wife have come to Milltown. Bongo players are extemporizing in the square. It's for peace, apparently. And, let's face it: if unmusical percussion doesn't make George W reconsider his foreign options, then nothing will. We don't know what they do to the enemy, but by God these drummers frighten *us*.

St Cadbury's Day represents the first chance this year for people to don the Ray Bans, get those tyres smoking and make a thorough nuisance of themselves in a semi-rural environment. There's always an appreciative audience for anyone attempting a handbrake turn, at speed, in St Bernard's Square. And Milltown is the ideal place to crank up the bass on that new in-car stereo and see what it'll do. As anyone living within five miles of Milltown is painfully aware, it sounds like a man armed with a leg of lamb trying to break out of an IKEA wardrobe.

There are two kinds of motorists who feel drawn, this Easter, to explore the narrow, twisty lanes around Milltown. There are those who want to pootle around at a stately 20mph ("Oh look, dear, a cow. And there, if I'm not mistaken, is another one". "More tea, dear?" "I don't mind if I do"), and those who see the South Pennine hills as a race-track, their very own Indianapolis 500. The prospect of these fruitcakes sharing the same stretch of road is a convincing argument for Milltown folk to stay home, draw the curtains and watch a re-run of The Italian Job on the telly. Compared with the motoring mayhem around Milltown, those Mini drivers are paragons of courtesy.

For a few hours St Bernard's Square is transformed into an impromptu display of classic motor-bikes. And, a few yards away, lounging on the benches outside the pub, is an impromptu display of classic motor-*bikers*. Close up, clad in leather, their helmets shining in the afternoon sunshine, they look like black beetles. It's a baffling aspect of biker life that they should decide, as one, to descend on a small South Pennine town, park up their bikes in the square, and sit around chatting to each other about... oh, all sorts, but mostly bikes. Yes, lock up your daughters, the Hell's Angels are here.

They ride good British bikes (none of your Japanese rubbish) that sound like an artillery barrage and drip oil all over the road. And – something of a Milltown specialty, this – huge three-wheeled behemoths, built out of khaki Meccano and scrapyard spares. Bedecked with jerry cans, they look as though they're ready for a trip across the Gobi Desert, or a location shoot for a post-apocalyptic Mad Max type movie... instead of just nipping into Milltown for a packet of Benson's and an hour or two of discreet posing.

To hear some of the locals talk – in hushed whispers – you'd think we'd been invaded by aliens. The bikers' reputation goes before them, but they're not as young as they were. There's no pressing need to lock up your daughters; maybe just keep granny indoors. And when the day is done they'll gun those bikes all the way home, through narrow Pennine lanes. They'll make a few old ladies jump, oh yes.

✢ ✢ ✢

The Green Weekend has come and gone. It's become one of the most important dates in the Milltown calendar – almost on a par with Hash Wednesday. The weekend was a great success, by all accounts. Shopkeepers and café proprietors appreciated the extra business (even those who'd happily vote for nuclear power and badger baiting) at a time of year when there's not much else going on. There was quite a run on bobble hats. Giant Rizlas couldn't be had for love nor money. And a bloke with a pedal-powered rickshaw was doing good business by ferrying people from one end of Sir Bernard's Square to the other. He had to take two fat lasses and a week's shopping halfway up Heartbreak Hill; that wiped the smile off his face.

Local pressure groups had stalls in the square. Why pay exorbitant heating bills, the crowds were asked, when they could harness the power of the sun? And, yes, solar power might seem to make sense in a place like Milltown, what with its sunny winters and Mediterranean-type climate. But the truth is rather different. We've got to face up to the fact, no matter how unpalatable it may be, that solar power is just not as sustainable as the tree-huggers like to suggest. If you leave your solar powered torch on charge by mistake, the next day will be cloudy and dull. Just coincidence? Hardly.

And if you listen to some of those cock-eyed optometrists we hear so much about, wave power is being touted as the Next Big Thing.[1] Poppycock. The seas *do* have their part to play in the future of the planet, of course they do, but not for creating energy. We need *somewhere* to put all that sewage. You could probably make a more convincing argument for bovine flatulence. The methane emitted by the world's population of cows would meet all our energy needs, apparently, and the only problem in harnessing this untapped source of energy is the painfully obvious one.

---

[1] Reservations about harnessing the power of the sea were expressed as early as 1870, when a paper on alternative forms of energy was presented to the Royal Society by a Professor Roderick Lumb. "Mark my words. Once we have sucked all the energy out of the waves, the oceans of the world will be as calm as millponds. Steam powers the mills that create the wealth for this great nation, and I can foresee a time when steam power will also be available in our homes. Imagine: a steam-powered way of toasting bread, or a steam-powered bedside light." The idea of a steam-powered toaster appealed to the scientific community and the general public alike. In 1870 people usually made toast over an open fire. Those who hadn't got a fire made toast by leaving slices of bread out in the sun: a time-consuming chore.

We were told that the Men of the Trees would make an appearance over the Green Weekend. But they had to cancel (a bad experience with a blackthorn, apparently) and their place was taken by the Men of the Shrubs, a shadowy organisation with paramilitary links to the Men of the Hardy Perennials. A short address by arboreal activist, Theresa Green, asked us all to think twice about felling trees. "Would we cut trees down so blithely if we could hear them screaming?", she asked. Well, we might, if they screamed all night and kept us awake.

Another raving harpy was laying into the fur trade, with some misguided guff about donkey jackets. "Think of the poor donkeys", she bleated. But no-one mistreats donkeys any more. Even the Spanish – a people not noted for their animal welfare – have stopped throwing donkeys out of belltowers during their fetes and ferias. The donkey-throwing business has – quite literally – gone underground. Now they throw donkeys down lift-shafts, which allows British holidaymakers to work on their tans without having their sensitivities disturbed. A good result all round.

Of course, once you advertise a Green Weekend, you tend to attract the lunatic fringe too. A 'Honk if You Love Peace and Quiet' campaign had a mixed reception. And the 'Put The Landfill Site Where The Poor People Live' petition is yet to reap rewards. But give it time. Let's be straight about this. "Looking after the planet for future generations" makes a useful, if meaningless, slogan. It's done the nuclear industry no harm. But we'd be more concerned about saving the planet if these self-appointed 'greens' could answer just one simple question: what the hell have those future generations ever done for *us*?

❖ ❖ ❖

Bill, our tourism officer, is reviewing all his strategies for attracting visitors to the area. As slogans go, 'Come to Milltown, You'll Like It' is beginning to look a bit lame. Suddenly the light bulb above his head comes on, and Bill scribbles furiously on the back of an envelope. He settles back in his revolving chair to admire his handiwork. 'Magnificent Milltown: where the present meets the past and makes an elegant swallow dive into the future'. You have to admit it's a masterpiece.

Sometimes we wonder why the visitors come, but who cares as long as we're robbing them blind. And, anyway, it's not really robbery as long as they're happy to spend money on some small souvenir of their day-trip to Milltown, like a didgeridoo or food poisoning. So the least we can do is organise a few events to facilitate the honourable process of fool/money separation.

You could go a long way (well, another postal district, anyway) to find better entertainment than our monthly car boot sales. Here, in the bargain basement of budget retailing, there's plenty of stuff to keep the browsers busy. 'Antiques of tomorrow', as the stallholders say: what used to be described, more prosaically, as 'rubbish'. Displayed artlessly on makeshift stalls is the kind of junk that most Milltown folk would be taking down to the dump: chipped coronation mugs, dodgy videos, old biscuit tins, novelty ashtrays, rusty tools and that elusive third LP by Bucks Fizz. Those who have suffered the misfortune of having their car radio nicked may find a replacement on one of the stalls. They may even find the one that was nicked in the first place.

As if that wasn't excitement enough, we hold the annual World Dock Pudding Championships. Despite its origins as an elaborate joke during the reign of Queen Victoria, cooking with weeds is taken very seriously round here. The competition is to see who can rustle up the best portion of this delicious local delicacy – so delicious, indeed, that we eat it just once a year.[2]

---

[2] The classic recipe was found by chance, hand-written on a scrap of paper tucked inside a slightly foxed first edition of Edwin Drudge's classic volume, *A Springtime Ramble in the Vale of the Calder*. 'Take 2 lbs young dock leaves, 1 2 lb nettle tops and 2 chopped onions. Boil everything in salted water. Add one cup of oatmeal, and cook for 20 minutes. Strain off liquid, stir in a knob of butter. Shape into puddings and fry in bacon fat. Throw puddings away. Eat out'. And, despite the intense rivalry on the day of the competition, this is the recipe that locals prefer.

The Pace Egg Play takes place on Good Friday. It's brilliant. Imagine what one of William Shakespeare's plays might have been like, if the bard of Stratford had gone unerringly for two-dimensional characters and undemanding jokes, and sensibly condensed two hours of overwrought action into a crowd-pleasing twenty minutes.

This ancient mummers' play recreates the classic combat between the forces of good (St George) and evil (foreigners, mostly), with a few other themes – jingoism, quack medicine, rank xenophobia, bringing the dead back to life, etc – thrown in for good measure. The host of splendid characters includes Bold Slasher, the Doctor (with his restorative bottle of Nip Nap), the King of Egypt, Osama Bin Laden and, best of all, a ragged, toothless *idiot savant* called Toss Pot.

Confusingly, two versions of the Pace Egg Play take place on the same day. The so-called 'boring' version is recommended for those of a nervous disposition. During the more violent, 'combat' version, however, the players have been known to let their natural exuberance run away with them. They may be a little hesitant during the first performance of the day. But by the time they've had a few beers, the strolling players are so exuberant they can hardly stand, never mind stroll. The script can get left behind as they improvise scenes of personal abuse and random violence. We hope there will be no repeat of the tragic events of 1987, when two spectators were accidentally stabbed to death during an altercation between St George and the Dragon over who was getting the beers in.

The Milltown and District Agricultural Show ('featuring the best of local produce since 1894') was another hardy annual, traditionally held on the first wet Sunday in June. It was a mid-summer extravaganza that promised something for everybody. That's what the poster said, anyway. To the show committee it was a Family Fun Day, though you had to think twice about any event that included the words 'Family' and 'Fun' in the same sentence. Offcumdens, doubtless used to more sophisticated fare, dubbed it the 'fete worse than death'.

A field just outside Milltown was transformed, for one day each year, into a rural playground filled with marquees, stalls and show-rings. It was our local squire, Lord Saveloy, who cut the ribbon and declared the show open. With the aristocracy losing most of its traditional perks (even deflowering virgins wasn't something they could take for granted any more), opening the show was Lord Saveloy's last public duty.

We enjoyed daring displays of derring-do by the Purple Helmets, Milltown's very own motor-cycle stunt team. They risked life and limb by jumping over a line of cars. But audiences weaned on big-budget blockbuster films soon got jaded, so the stakes had to be raised with each performance. One year the team attempted the stunt while towing a caravan, giving the crowd what they came for... that's assuming they'd come to witness a lethal fireball.

The Milltown Show was an opportunity for the local farmers to get together and monopolise the bar in the beer tent. Once they'd been let off the leash for the day, they could put a fair few pints away. When they emerged, blinking into the afternoon sunshine, they'd cast covetous eyes over the brand-new tractors on display. They tried to convince themselves their work-rate would increase if they had heated seats, double-glazed windows and a state-of-the-art in-cab CD system... to replace the clapped-out tractors rusting away on the farm.

The vicar's wife used to run the childrens' pet show. When picking a winner, it would have taken the wisdom of Solomon to choose between the rival claims of, say, a guinea pig and a shaggy shetland pony. So, since they were all God's creatures, every pet got a rosette. Kids could toss ping-pong balls into buckets, and hope to win a goldfish. It was a convenient way to teach children about pet-care and mortality, often on the same day.

The Milltown Show was a pleasantly old-fashioned affair. In the main tent we could admire the displays of fruit, vegetables and home-made produce. The competition categories were reassuringly traditional; so it was 'three English apples', 'six broad beans' and 'pot of home-made lemon curd'... rather than 'three mobile phones' or 'six website portals'. The children exhibited woven samplers, and examples of their neatest handwriting. Their models were made, in best Blue Peter style, out of toilet rolls, washing-up bottles and sticky-back plastic. The 'guess the weight of the cake' competition was nearly cancelled one year, when a goat ate the cake. It took a sudden and triumphant leap of imagination to change the name of the competition to 'guess the weight of the goat'.

Yes, when we saw the marquees going up in Potter's Field, we felt a sense of community that stretched back as far as anyone could remember. So it's a real shame that the Milltown and District Agricultural Show became a casualty of the foot and mouth epidemic. The show was cancelled last year (the first time since the Second World War) and God only knows when it will be held again.

We've tried all sorts of events, over the years, to bring tourists into town. Book-burning, for example: a fine old tradition that's rather fallen out of fashion since the collapse of the Third Reich. Our aim was to resurrect the idea in a modern context, feeling that the collected works of Lord Archer[3] would make a damn good blaze.

The Victorian Weekend enjoyed a brief vogue; from dawn to dusk you could hardly move for crippled children, unfrocked vicars and women of easy virtue. We've had beer festivals – even though, for most folk, the prospect of '200 real ales, ciders and perries' on sale

---

[3] Novels, short stories and Jeffrey's forthcoming prison diary 'Bubba and Me, a love forged in adversity'. The book will detail the demanding relationship with his cellmate, a man with a low IQ but an unimpaired sex drive. It couldn't have happened to a nicer guy.

in a draughty marquee is about 195 too many. The Festival of Sarcasm ("Yeah, right, what a great idea *that* was") came and went, largely unlamented. One year we had a Festival of Shoplifting but, to be honest, it's something we'd rather forget about.

Given the town's relaxed attitude to paternity, Father's Day is proving to be a real money-spinner. After all, if kids send one Father's Day card, they're as likely to send half a dozen. And Sperm Donor's Day was a noble attempt to 'Remember the anonymous man who gave you the gift of life'. In hindsight, though, we shouldn't have printed so many cards. What's next on the agenda? Surrogate Mother's Day, perhaps, to celebrate some unsung heroines. If nothing else it might give the manufacturers of turkey basters something to cheer about.

✥ ✥ ✥

All these events pale into insignificance, though, compared to the Milltown Mardi Gras. It started off in the most modest way – really just to add a little colour to the gaunt gritstone scene – but we think we may be onto a winner. Despite media reports about Milltown being the Lesbian Capital of the North, we recognised that lesbianism is merely one of many possible sexual orientations. And not every guy in town is gay (or "waiting for the right girl", as we used to say). He may simply be light on his feet.

We wanted to raise the profile of a beleaguered minority. People who feel drawn to express their sexuality in a traditional way. People who might not otherwise feel they had a great deal to shout about. That, in a nutshell, was the origin of the Straight Pride March. It seemed an inspired idea – giving heterosexual folk the chance to reclaim the streets, stand shoulder to shoulder and let the world know they existed. "Say it out loud... We're straight and we're proud". We even have a prize for the best outfit, the Breeders' Cup ('bring proof of sexual orientation', the brochure stipulates, without suggesting exactly what that might be). Yes, if there's another South Pennine town that celebrates the multi-facetted nature of heterosexuality by dressing up in gaudy costumes, then we've never heard of it.

There's more to the Mardi Gras weekend that just marching, though. Last year, for example, we took the theme of 'Ogling'. We wanted to celebrate that defining moment of truth when young guys suddenly realise that underneath their clothes all women are totally naked. Men are encouraged to objectify women by reducing them to their constituent body parts. "Just *look* at the arse on that...". But let's be specific: when a guy reckons "You don't get many of *them* to the kilo", exactly *how many* to the kilo are we talking about? We made it into a competition that we hoped would be 'fun for all the family'.[4]

We organised an evening of 'Pole and Lap Dancing' – assuming, naturally enough, that the agency would send us a couple of good-looking lasses who were prepared to perform all manner of degrading sexual acts in the guise of harmless entertainment. Maybe a little girl-on-girl action, too, if the atmosphere was conducive. Great ogling opportunities, we thought, for shy men whose only contact with attractive women was a bit of harmless frottage on a crowded bus. What we actually ended up with was 'Pole and *Lapp* Dancing', not the same thing at all. One of the women – she looked as though she'd be more at home tossing hot rivets in the shipyards of Gdansk – swayed listlessly to a slow polka. The other lass – pleasant enough, but wrapped from head to foot in animal skins – performed an interminable dance that celebrated the return of the reindeer to the Arctic tundra.

We tried to withhold payment; a breach of promise was mentioned. The women would have none of it. Though she could speak only a few words of English, the Polish lady illustrated, in a most graphic way, that she was able to crush a man's head between her thighs until it burst like an over-ripe watermelon. Then she insisted on cash. We won't be using that agency again.

---

[4] The prize was a copy (video or DVD) of 'Gumshot Cavalcade': a pioneering effort in bringing Busby Berkeley-style dance routines to the genre of hard-core porn.

This year we're planning a rather more sombre occasion, provisionally entitled A Requiem for the G-spot. For years men have been encouraged – nay, badgered – to search for it, even though we didn't really know what we were looking for, or where we might find it, or whether we'd recognise it even if we we *did* happen to come across it. But searching for the G-spot was reckoned to be 'a good thing', proving to his partner that a man could look beyond his own selfish needs. And if the G-spot had to be found, then, by golly, we were prepared to roll up our sleeves and give it our best shot. We deserved a medal – for persistence, at least. How many evenings of frustration began with a guy setting off on a G-spot safari? It seemed a mammoth undertaking, like trying to find the source of the Nile, or the North West Passage... *and* doing it blindfolded.

So it's hurtful to be told now that the G-spot doesn't even exist. It was a wild goose chase, guys. Just another lie, like 'size doesn't matter' and the whole idea of 'living happily ever after'. The reason we couldn't find it isn't because we weren't trying hard enough. We couldn't find the little devil because it wasn't actually *there*. Have we received any kind of apology? Have we hell... Not even a shrug of the shoulders and a mildly embarrassed "Sorry", at having wasted so much of our time, energy and goodwill. *Pah*...

The Milltown Mardi Gras allows people to express their sexuality in a more public way than they might be accustomed to. When he loses his virginity, a man may want to share his good fortune – perhaps by making a triumphant tour of the town in an open-topped bus. Another man may choose to stand at the end of his street, hands on hips, and announce to the world: "I, Stanley Peregrine Gawkroger, have pleasured my woman". We may decide to demonstrate our solidarity with the cause of gay pride by having casual sex in public toilets. Or we may wear badges – 'How dare you assume I'm homosexual' – in an attempt to challenge over-hasty stereotyping. A couple might give a demonstration of Tantric sex, a technique by which a man can postpone his orgasm for up to an hour. Maybe *two* hours if the couple take in a meal and a movie too.

On the buses

Our local train service is going to hell in a handcart. Having to spend hours waiting on draughty platforms for trains that don't arrive is making commuters stressed-out and fretful. Even RailTrack's exciting new slogan – 'Better late than never' – fails to improve their gloomy mood. No wonder that busy people are looking for alternative ways of getting to work. They can take the car out, of course, but the valley road is congested enough already. Add a few more hot-headed motorists and there'll be total gridlock.

In our imaginations, of course, the car represents freedom. We've all seen the adverts. We're driving along a deserted alpine road in a red sports car – the hood down, the wind in our hair, a gorgeous member of the opposite sex in the passenger seat who's lost in admiration of our driving skills. Suddenly the road is riven by an earthquake, or, worse, turns into a spitting cobra: driving conditions about which the Highway Code gives no advice whatsoever. We'll do anything to avoid admitting that we're really just joining a line of traffic stuttering slowly towards oblivion – car and driver fuming in unison. And then, when we eventually find a parking space, we hardly dare move the car for fear that we lose 'our' place. It's a strange kind of freedom.

Cycling to work is a good idea, in theory. In practise, however, cycling reinforces the notion of life as a lottery, with an accident blackspot at every turn. Cars and cyclists have the same kind of relationship as bulls and china shops; the further apart they are kept, the better. No-one gives way to cyclists – or 'organ donors', as they're known down at the A & E Department. Even when they take refuge in bus-lanes, they have to share them with taxis and buses: the cyclists' natural predators. Sudden death is never more than a heartbeat away.

Then there's the clobber to consider. It's an 'all or nothing' kind of deal these days. You can't just go for a bike ride, you've got to buy into the whole cycling schtick. If you wear something sensible, you'll be shunned by other cyclists. If you wear what *they* wear (a helmet that looks like a pound of over-ripe bananas and figure-hugging Lycra in a variety of day-glo colours, embellished with a stripe of mud all the way up the back) you'll be openly mocked by everybody else. Prat or pariah: never an easy choice to make. If you weave in and out of stationary traffic, you'll make an enemy of every car driver you pass. Since drivers have long memories, short fuses and a pathological loathing of Lycra louts, you'll be storing up trouble for yourself.

Instead of risking life and limb on the roads, you can safely recreate the cycling experience indoors. Ride an exercise bike, activate the sprinkler system and get family and friends to poke their heads round the door every few seconds to shout abuse at you.

Why wobble about on two wheels when you can catch a bus instead? If you just want to get to town, be assured that there'll be a bus along every twenty minutes. So far so good, except that buses suffer from a major image problem. Travelling by bus is a rather too accurate indicator of social standing, winnowing the wheat from the chaff. Motorists look at buses in the same way that our great-grandparents looked at the workhouse: in fear and trepidation that one day they too might be reduced to this most public admission of defeat. Petrol would have to be £100 a litre before drivers would consider giving up the sheer convenience of sitting in a traffic jam with hundreds of other cars, drumming impatient fingers on leatherette dashboards. They'd rather *push* the damn car to work than be seen catching a bus.

A bus is not a viable option for busy go-getters – with places to go, people to do and deadlines to meet. If a businessman with a briefcase were to get on a bus, he might just as well wear a badge on his lapel reading 'I've been sacked, my company car's been taken back and I'm on my way to the Job Club. Kill me now, please, it would be a kindness'. Your average businessman would rather stand naked in the company car-park, being flicked remorselessly with wet towels, than be forced to spend a single second sitting on a bus. It's the ultimate humiliation.

Newcomers to bus travel need to be tutored in bus etiquette. Even choosing where to sit requires a little care. You might imagine you can sit wherever you like, but this is not quite true. The bus is, albeit invisibly, segregated into different sections. On top it's kids at the front, smirking teenagers at the back, with adults – mostly hacking smokers – in the middle. On the bottom it's mostly old folk and the mad, with the oldest and most infirm towards the front. There is just enough space by the door for one boring arsehole – male, middle-aged, with a comb-over – to stand all the way into town and make small-talk to the driver.

It's an uneasy mixture. The old folk look at the kids and regret their own lost youth, so long ago, when they still had most of their marbles. Seeing these kids – so boisterous and carefree – just adds insult to old age. Why *do* the kids have to make such a damn racket all the time? And that so-called music they listen to... It's not music, it's just a noise. The kids barely notice the old folk at all. They might conclude "Oh my God, that's what *I'll* be like one day", but they are spared such gloomy thoughts by the happy conviction that they are immortal and that old age is something that happens to other people, and not to them at all.

There is, please note, no first class section on a bus: no convenient demarcation between the riff-raff and the chosen few. There's nowhere for a man in a pin-striped suit to sit and work at his laptop. Nowhere to spread out a spreadsheet. Nowhere to get a cup of coffee and a sandwich. Nowhere to escape the overpowering smell of parma violets and piss. But the social niceties of bus travel don't end there. For example, do you sit next to someone you've been chatting to in the bus queue? To do so might seem a little forward, while not to do so might be seen as stand-offish. Or maybe you're sitting next to someone on a crowded bus which almost empties at one stop. Should you now move to a new seat – and risk offending your neighbour – or stay where you are, wedged so tightly together that you can't even cross your legs? We need a manual of our own – *Debrett's Guide to Omnibus Etiquette*, perhaps – to help us mind our manners.

With the valley road being dug up every few days, the Milltown run is viewed by the bus drivers as a punishment for poor timekeeping. If they want to get their regular routes back, they'll have to follow the bus drivers' handbook to the letter. This requires them to accelerate as fast as possible from every bus-stop, then braking equally hard at the next one – thus making the journey as uncomfortable as possible for their passengers. With a glance in the mirror and a well-timed tap-dancing routine on the gas pedal and the brake, they can transfer an old biddy and her tartan shopping trolley from one end of the bus to the other in less time than it takes to say "Hold tight at the back". It's moments like these that make a bus driver's life worthwhile.

It's a pity that buses are so maligned. OK, they're mundane and utilitarian, but they get the job done. They just don't inspire obsessive devotion, in the way that, say, bikes do. Otherwise these old biddies would be taking buses out to some scruffy café, in the middle of nowhere, with tables and chairs bolted to the lino floor, where they'd congregate in noisy groups, slurping strong tea from chipped mugs and talking about... well, buses mostly.

In truth it can be fun to bounce around the country lanes in a bus – at least for those blessed with strong constitutions and with few constraints upon their time. The rural routes are in decline ("What's that big red thing, dad?" "It's a bus, lad. Take a good long look; it may be the last you see round here") so go on, catch a country bus while you still can.

As soon as the bus-drivers venture off the main road and take to the hills, the normal rules of bus travel are suspended for the duration of the trip. Forget whatever you've read in the timetable, especially the length of time your journey might take. Don't be lulled into any false sense of security by the idea that the bus is only going a few miles. The country lanes above Milltown are unmapped, labyrinthine, bereft of signs; even locals get lost. Roads can come to a sudden end at a muddy farmyard, or deteriorate into a cart-track that heads off God knows where. Some of the bus-drivers have such a poor sense of direction that they have to to stop periodically and ask for directions. It's not unknown for the drivers to organise a whip-round to fill the tank up, when they've run out of petrol.

You'll need provisions. Imagine you're embarking on an African safari, and pack accordingly. At the very least, you should take some refreshments for the outward leg. If you're attacked by crazed pensioners, suffering from hunger and acute tannin deprivation, you may be able to hold them off with some cheese & pickle sandwiches and a flask of milky tea. In extremis, a bag of Werthers Original might do the trick. Wear a scarf or cravat over your face; it will help to keep out the dust and the flies and the overpowering smell of lavender water. By the time the bus rolls into Milltown once again, having covered half the county, most of the passengers will be delirious. No wonder the rural routes have been re-classified as white-knuckle rides. You have been warned.

Saint Bernard's head

We spent a small fortune, a couple of years ago, on what we were reliably informed was a solar powered sundial. It seemed an appropriate way to commemorate the Millennium. It was only when we'd put it up, at one end of St Bernard's Square, that some bright spark enlightened us to the fact that *every* sundial is solar powered. Yes, there was no getting away from it: we'd been had. And every time we saw that accursed sundial, it just served to remind us how silly we'd been. So we took it down, and the mayor is storing it in his basement until we can find some other use for it. In any case, why would anyone want to remember the Millennium? It's been and gone. Good riddance, we say.

That unfortunate episode should have taught us a lesson. Nevertheless, a lot of people were keen that Milltown should mark the Queen's Jubilee of 2002 with something more tangible than a monumental hangover. There was no shortage of ideas – good, bad and indifferent. We could have banned cars from the square and opened it up to pedestrians. That was a good idea. We could have erected a statue of St Bernard, Milltown's very own Purley King, in grateful thanks for everything he has done for the town.[1] That was a bad idea.[2] And most people in town are utterly indifferent... to St Bernard, the monarchy *and* the Jubilee. Are the pubs open yet?

Some kind of memorial would be found, no doubt. But with the coffers nearly empty after that sundial shambles, we needed to

---

[1] After all, he did the decent thing and fucked off fifty years ago. Imagine the nightmare scenario. He could having been living in Milltown all this time. He could be living down your street... maybe next door to you. It makes you think.

[2] We should, instead, be following the sterling example set by Madame Tussauds. They've melted down their figure of St Bernard, recycling the wax to create the England World Cup squad and a *tableau vivant* of Hannibal crossing the Alps. The elephants are quite a crowd-puller, apparently. From St Bernard's jowls alone they managed to make Britney Spears. Such is the transitory nature of celebrity. *Sic transit gloria mundi*.

raise more money. The traditional method is to rattle a collecting tin under the noses of drinkers while they're enjoying a pint in the pubs of Milltown. The well-heeled patrons of the Stoic will dip their hands in their pockets if a tin is rattled loud and long enough. But it's a strange irony that the rougher the pub, the more money the regulars seem to raise for charity. And few pubs in the Milltown area are rougher that the Grievous Bodily Arms. It's the sort of pub where bogus MOT certificates can be had for the price of a pint. And if you win more than 50p on the fruit machine, the biggest problem is getting out alive. But when it comes to charity, you only have to mention children or animals to have big men with broken noses getting dewy-eyed and sentimental.

They'll peel fivers from suspiciously thick wads of notes, eased out of back pockets. They'll build piles of pennies on the bar. They'll participate in all kinds of sponsored events – especially if they involve feats of brute strength or dressing up in women's clothing. So when the landlord suggested a duck race, to raise money for the jubilee fund, the idea went down a storm. Even after learning that no real ducks would be involved, the regulars were happy to muck in.

They bought three thousand yellow plastic ducks from a place that specialised in bulk sales of yellow plastic ducks; it's amazing what you can find in the Yellow Pages. Every duck had a different number painted on its bottom, and visitors and locals alike were encouraged to 'buy' one. Sales were as buoyant as the ducks themselves, thanks to the terrific prizes donated by local businesses. First prize: a thirty-second trolley dash around the Twig Shop. Wow… some lucky winner will never need to buy twigs and fir-cones again. Second prize: a free session with a visiting chiropodist. Third prize: dinner for two at the Grievous Bodily Arms (cutlery not included). By the time the great day arrived, all the ducks had been spoken for. So far, so good.

Our river is a watercourse of many moods: a mere trickle in high summer, a roaring torrent after winter rain. Sometimes it misbehaves – like when it sluiced through our lovely homes. But mostly it goes quietly about its business.

On the day of the Duck Race, crowds lined both sides of the river in eager anticipation. The river looked low, but no-one seemed to be overly concerned about that. A net was stretched taut between the stanchions of the old packhorse bridge – the finishing line – to catch the ducks as they completed the course. Two hundred yards upstream, where the road crosses the river, a tipper truck full of ducks was backed over the parapet. On an agreed signal, three thousand yellow ducks slid from the back of the truck and hit the water simultaneously.

The event, as a genuine race, was over there and then. The breeze, though light, was still stronger than the river's sluggish current. Instead of rushing pell-mell downstream, in the approved manner, three thousand yellow ducks closed ranks – in a jaundiced armada – and sullenly refused to move. The breeze quickened, pushing ducks to the water margins, where they got stuck in the reeds and the branches of overhanging trees.

After half an hour, a few dozen ducks had floated as far as the weir by the old mill. But instead of taking the plunge, the ducks floated around in ever-decreasing circles. After an hour of surreal inactivity, the crowd began to get restless. A few people decided they had better things to do with their time than watch a river. Little kids, blessed with a low boredom threshold, demanded chips and ice cream. People started to throw stones: some to dislodge ducks, others for devilment. Stewards in yellow tabards waded into the water and tried to hurry the ducks along. They fell over and got drenched; people laughed; words were exchanged. The ducks remained stubbornly uncooperative, their identical expressions no longer cute but mocking: Stepford Ducks.

A few ducks eventually crossed the finishing line, but only because they'd been thrown there. "It's a fix", shouted the few onlookers who hadn't already drifted away in disillusionment. "That's the last duck race *we'll* ever go to". What a shambles.

The following week the *Milltown Times* printed this statement from an ashen-faced Duck Race spokesman, who asked to remain anonymous. "It is difficult to know what to say about the shameful events of last weekend. We are stunned. The entire duck-racing community is stunned. We have witnessed many sporting disasters in recent years. The abortive Grand National of 1993. Mike Tyson chewing Evander Holyfield's ear off. Derek Pringle. And – most recently and most sadly – Halifax Town being relegated from Division 3 into the barren wastes of the Conference League. But these are as nothing compared to the duck debacle of Easter Monday.

"The river level was unseasonably low, making the going firmer than we (or the ducks) would have liked. Some people in the crowd suggested the ducks weren't trying, though random drug tests proved negative until we started on the onlookers. After all, it was their boos and catcalls which disorientated the ducks and made them swim around in circles. I am not making excuses; no-one comes out of this fiasco with much dignity. There will be a steward's enquiry. Heads will roll. Thank you".

Beneath this terse statement was a display ad: "Almost 3,000 plastic ducks for sale. Nearly new. No sensible offer refused".

The winning duck, incidentally, was number 69 – bought, perhaps unfortunately, by the landlord of the Grievous Bodily Arms himself. Given the resulting outcry he acted honourably in deciding not to take up his prize, but to raffle it at a later date. In the meantime he has decided to take a short holiday, and will not be available for further comment about the Duck Race or, indeed, anything else.

Right to roam

Bill, Milltown's tourism officer, is feeling rather pleased with himself. And why shouldn't he? A two-day brainstorming session (with Bill and his staff holed up, at the council's expense, in a rather splendid four-star hotel) has produced a host of new visitor initiatives. After so many months of misery, it's vital that the rural economy gets a shot in the arm.

The session was a great success, with all local tourism initiatives now coming under one umbrella, 'Tourism 2002'. Everyone agreed that this name was catchy and up-to-date. The icing on the cake (black forest gateau, incidentally, and "rather good") was an exciting new slogan. 'Milltown: closer than you think... if you live nearby': that should do the trick. Bill rewarded himself with an Irish coffee for dreaming that one up. The other candidate - 'Milltown: Yorkshire's Best-kept Secret' - appeared to contain a subliminal criticism of the tourism department, and was voted down, five to four, after second helpings from the sweet trolley. Yes, however much that brainstorming shindig cost, it was money well spent.

Farmers had it tough, when foot and mouth ravaged the landscape. We watched in horror as cows were piled onto funeral pyres - a sight that evoked a host of uncomfortable associations. The hill farmers had our sympathies. It can't have been easy to stand by and watch as their animals were slaughtered. It would have been like witnessing the death of a much-loved member of the family: a much-loved member of the family with a one-way ticket to the abattoir.

Walkers did the decent thing. They obeyed the footpath restrictions and stayed away from livestock. They put their walking boots away. It seemed a small price to pay if it would help to wipe the disease off the map. But foot and mouth damn near wiped out the tourist trade too.

As visitor numbers plummeted, Bill clutched at straws. He organised a series of town walks, in the rather desperate hope that ramblers would come all the way to Milltown, lace up their boots and join a group of cagoule-clad plodders to explore the highlights of a small, South Pennine town - including the fire station, the Co-op car-park and the boggy end of the cricket pitch (described by Bill as 'A valuable wetland habitat for rare species. Mostly horseflies'). The first town walk set the tone for the rest. Since most ramblers don't like passing a pub without nipping in to try the beer, an intimate exploration of Milltown took eight hours, of which the last two were just a blur.

Terry was one local walker who went stir crazy while the countryside was out of bounds. The walls of his bijou Milltown hovel closed in a little more with every day that passed. Armed with an economy tin of dubbin, he vented his frustrations on his walking boots. They haven't been this clean since the salesman first took them out of the box. They've been sitting in the hallway, tongues out, like a pair of obedient dogs waiting patiently for walkies. Terry's cagoule was hung nearby, where he last left it. Finding a prawn salad sandwich in the breast pocket solved a problem that had public health inspectors foxed for months.

✣ ✣ ✣

The sign that greeted motorists – 'Milltown welcomes careful drivers' – was taken down last year. We didn't see the point in alienating crap drivers. After all, even the most accident-prone drivers have cash to spend, and the pubs, cafés and guest-houses of Milltown didn't want to miss out. If the National Association of Reckless Drivers (and Affiliated Operatives in the Bus and Taxi Businesses) had wanted to hold their AGM and dinner dance in Milltown, all we would have said was "When and where?" Yes, that's how bad things were round here.

Thankfully, those dark days are now behind us. The worst outbreak of foot and mouth since the last one has been declared dead and buried, along with more than four million cattle, sheep and pigs. The countryside is 'open for business' again, whatever that's supposed to mean. We waited for the visitors to return - fingers poised over the cash-tills like typists waiting for dictation - and our faith seems to be justified. Tourism 2002 is exceeding expectations. A record number of tourist brochures were dispatched - each and every one a triumph of anodyne banality - and bookings are well up on last year.

Spring is here, bringing new life, new hope. If a South Pennine winter is like being hermetically sealed inside a Tupperware container, then spring is like an unseen hand prising the lid off. We feel free, emancipated. There are sights to cheer the most jaded souls. Colour is returning to the landscape, like the blush to a maiden's cheek. The grass is greening up and the fields have the look of brushed moleskin. It's idyllic, the nearest we get to a vision of Eden. Trees are laden down with blossom; from a distance it looks like freshly popped popcorn. The gritstone scene is softened - for a few days, at least - by the candy-floss colours of spring. Milltown looks its very best. We'd best enjoy it while we can; the town won't look this good again for another 11 1/2 months.

The harsh spring light makes a searching examination of our lives too, with rather more clarity than we either need or want. We feel a strong urge to shake ourselves out of our lethargy. And, with our failings and foibles mercilessly exposed, this is a good opportunity to take stock. New Year is no time to make life-changing resolutions; the time for self-improvement is *now*.

This is the time to get fit, to keep those promises to walk down to the paper shop instead of just taking the car. Pessimists can watch the blossom blow away in the first stiff breeze. It reinforces what they already know, that good things don't last. Optimists, on the other hand, can pack a rucksack with sandwiches and Kendal Mint Cake, take a deep breath and set out to enjoy a ramble in the sweet springtime air. There's nothing like a bracing hike for putting pressing difficulties into some kind of perspective. A walk won't make problems evaporate, like the morning mist burnt off by summer sun. They'll still be there when you get home, but maybe they won't loom quite so large.

Walking has a pleasantly analgesic effect, there's no doubt about it. It's relaxing to walk on sheep-cropped grass instead of unresponsive Tarmac. We can be profligate with our time instead of 'managing' it. We can wander aimlessly over the tops instead of subjecting ourselves to a route march. We can gives ourselves up to the sights, sounds and smells of the countryside, before nipping into a pub, *en route*, to give the other two senses a bit of a workout. That's what Bill's going to do this weekend. Mind you, he's already planning another departmental get-together - maybe a long weekend just after Christmas, somewhere a little closer to Alton Towers - to dream up another snappy name for the unseemly clamour to claim the tourism pound. 'Tourism 2003' is an early favourite, but let's not be too hasty.

❖ ❖ ❖

While foot and mouth was keeping walkers off the tops, there were slim pickings down at Take a Hike, Milltown's premier retail outlet for walking accoutrements. The gaffer had a face as long as a Pennine winter. Now, though, there's a spring in his step and a glint in his eye. He rubs his hands expectantly, especially when Terry comes through the door.

There was a time - it seems so long ago - when walking was a very simple activity. You'd just slip on something shapeless and warm, and put one foot in front of the other. Now, of course, we scorn such a miserly approach. We're happy to spend folding money to ensure that we look the part. We used to buy a pair of boots or a rucksack; now we buy 'a system'. We used to pull on a mud-coloured windjammer, made from the same low-tech rain-attracting material from which they make bath sponges. Now we have smart, figure-hugging garments - in this year's tastefully co-ordinated colours, of course - which keep us striding through torrential rain long after the enjoyment has gone... just to see if a £250 cagoule really is as waterproof as the manufacturers suggest.

We used to find a forked stick and whittle it with a pen-knife. It was something to do while waiting for the kettle to boil in the kitchen of some blighted youth hostel. The result - after only a few hours of graft, and a couple of bandaged fingers - was a home-made walking-stick. Now we go to an outdoor shop instead and pick up a telescopic pole in lightweight titanium, with three sections and an ergonomic handle. And we spurn something as simple as a penknife, in favour of a Swiss Army Knife. Isn't it somehow typical of the Swiss that their army should be famous, not for a successful military campaign, but for precision-made cutlery?

You can still buy a Swiss Army Knife with just a couple of blades, but only a skinflint would be content with that. At Take a Hike the knives recline seductively in a display case. Like the brazen denizens of some red-light district, the pleasures become more exotic with every fiver you're prepared to pay: corkscrew, saw, screwdriver, magnifying glass and that pointy thing that no-one knows what to do with. Towards the top of the range - it's serious 'three-in-a-waterbed' money now - you get a watch, compass, hedge trimmer, arc-welder and full internet connection... plus a smart leather case on wheels to keep it in. You want one. You know you do. But if you have to ask the price, you really can't afford one.

Terry is a gadget junkie, and this is just the kind of stuff that makes his heart beat faster. He can't resist something new. New and matt-black is good. New, matt-black and insanely expensive is better. He likes to get away to the hills, if only to stop his wife castigating him for wasting their money on yet another spectacularly useless piece of frippery.

She badgers him to do something about their garden. By letting the grass grow proud and tall, and the flowers go to seed, Terry has convinced himself (though not, as yet, his neighbours) that he is creating a 'wildlife sanctuary'. A place where songbirds sing, and butterflies flit from flower to flower. A haven for rare species of slugs and biting insects. But Terry's not the kind of man to sit at home, waiting to be told what he should be doing. He'd rather be out on the fells, wowing the members of the walking club with his latest toys.

If your boots cost £50, then Terry's boots cost £100. If your walking stick has a compass in the handle, his walking stick could probably find its own way home. If your cagoule is showerproof, then his cagoule can sing in the rain and perform card tricks. "With this GPS (that's 'global positioning system' to you)", he says, "you can pinpoint your position on the globe to an accuracy of a few metres". But how does it work? "Haven't a clue", he admits, in a rare show of candour, tossing it back in his rucksack.

He's the proud owner of a digital altimeter. In the good old days a doomed mountaineer would consign his thoughts to paper: "Here I am, halfway up a mountain, and gangrene is setting in...". Now, armed with Terry's gadget, a mountaineer could be pedantically accurate, as he pens that last letter to his loved ones: "Here I am, at exactly 6,176 metres above sea-level, and gangrene is setting in...". Think what a comfort that could be.

✦ ✦ ✦

Better late than never, the right to roam is now on the statute books. Hooray! And let's give thanks to those hardy pioneers who faced dangers of their own, more than half a century ago, in helping to open up the hills to riff-raff like Terry. Hats off to those who took part in the Mass Trespass on Kinder, and other acts of civil disobedience. Without their stubborn resistance to rapacious landowners, Terry's rambles might still be limited to a few, over-used lowland paths - mostly between the bookies and the off-licence.

There are places he never knew he wanted to explore until someone told him he wasn't allowed to. Especially when he's denied access by some poncy landowner - Lord Saveloy, for example, the infamous sausage baron - who insists that walkers will damage his land. So let's get it straight: it's bobble-hatted ramblers who upset the delicate ecological balance of a grouse moor, rather than those hunting parties of Japanese businessmen who pay huge sums to blast the birds to kingdom come.

Landowners are happy to leap on the environmental bandwagon at every opportunity. But even in a class-obsessed country like ours, it is surely an indefensible anachronism for a small, titled elite to lay claim to vast tracts of our countryside. It's even worse when they try to keep country-lovers out. The British aristocracy should be grateful that we didn't follow the sterling example of Madame Guillotine. Instead of dispatching these pampered aristos two hundred years ago, we let the buggers live. Worse, we're happy to pay to visit their palaces and mansions, thereby keeping them in the luxury to which they've become accustomed over the centuries.

Should we really entrust the countryside to a landed gentry whose main qualification for the job seems to be the ability to drink cream sherry and talk in loud, braying voices? Their arrogance is breathtaking. Whenever Terry hears a spokesman for country landowners brand him and his kind as "A handful of rampant ramblers", his hands clench into fists. So it was quite a surprise when the Landed Gentry Association issued the following press release[1], in the form of an open letter to every person living in this green and pleasant land.

We, the members of the Landed Gentry Association of Great Britain, would like to express our heartfelt gratitude to you, the British public, for allowing us to survive for so many centuries. Frankly, we thought the game was up about the time of the French Revolution.

---

[1] We can dream, can't we?

We now appreciate that the upland tracts do not belong to us, in any real sense, and that we are but humble custodians, on your behalf, of these treasured landscapes. We feel pleased - nay, privileged - to have you on this land. We know how hard it is for you to take time off, in your busy lives, to come and visit us. We want you to come and visit us. We really do. We have waived all admission charges to our lovely homes. And if something catches your eye - a family portrait, perhaps, or a priceless Fabergé bauble - feel free to take it home with you as a small souvenir of your visit. We thank you one and all.

If you've enjoyed *The Todmorden Book of the Dead*, then maybe you'll like these other books too. Week by week, month by month, year by sodding year, the Milltown books build into an encyclopedia of South Pennine life that can only increase in value.

View From the Bridge, the first book in the series, received the ultimate accolade: being transformed by Arthur Miller into a successful stage play. The book began as - and remains - a 25,000-word love-song to a small, idiosyncratic milltown and the people who have made it their home. Since then it's been downhill all the way, with four further books being foisted upon an increasingly apathetic public.

View From the Bridge
£5.95, published by Pennine Pens,
ISBN 1-873378-47-5

Back to the Bridge
£4.95, published by Pennine Pens,
ISBN 1-873378-52-1

A Bridge Too Far
£4.95, published by Pennine Pens,
ISBN 1-873378-57-2

Women are from Venus, Men are from Mytholmroyd
£4.95, published by Mutton Stew,
ISBN 0-9538608-0-9